United States Presidents

Ronald Reagan

Series Consultant:
Don M. Coerver, professor of history
Texas Christian University, Fort Worth, Texas

Karen Judson

Enslow Publishers, Inc.

44 Fadem Road   PO Box 38
Box 699   Aldershot
Springfield, NJ 07081   Hants GU12 6BP
USA   UK

Copyright © 1997 by Karen Judson

Library of Congress Cataloging-in-Publication Data

Ronald Reagan / Karen Judson.
    p. cm. — (United States presidents)
      Includes bibliographical references and index.
    Summary: Traces the life and career of Ronald Reagan, from his childhood
in Illinois, through his time as an actor, to his activities in public office.
    ISBN 0-89490-835-9
    1. Reagan, Ronald—Juvenile literature. 2. Presidents—United
States—Biography—Juvenile literature. 3. Governors—California—
Biography—Juvenile literature. 4. Motion picture actors and actresses—
United States—Biography—Juvenile literature. 5. United States—Politics
and government—1981-1989—Juvenile literature. [1. Reagan, Ronald.
2. Presidents. 3. Actors and actresses.] I. Title. II. Series.
E877.J84 1997
973.927'092—dc20
    [B]   96-36482
                                                         CIP
                                                         AC

Printed in the United States of America

10 9 8 7 6 5 4 3 2 1

Illustration Credits: Ronald Reagan Library, pp. 12, 16, 19, 21, 32, 35, 51, 68, 71,
75, 77, 80, 87, 97.

Source Document Credits: California State Archives, pp. 42, 43, 46, 47; Ronald
Reagan Library, pp. 52, 60, 62, 63, 69, 73, 78, 86, 91, 96.

Cover Illustration: Ronald Reagan Library

Contents

1

THE HERO

O n Monday, March 30, 1981, Ronald Wilson Reagan had been President of the United States for sixty-nine days. At about 2:00 P.M. that day, President Reagan went to the Hilton Hotel in Washington, D.C., to speak to thirty-five hundred trade union members about his economic policies. The President dressed sharply for his speech in a crisp white shirt and a new blue suit. Many of the union members had voted against him in the election of 1980, so he hoped to make a good impression on them.

President Reagan's speech went well, and at 2:30 P.M., he left the Hilton Hotel. With him were several White House aides and the Secret Service agents and police officers assigned to protect him. The President and his party stepped out onto T Street, where limousines were waiting to return them to the White House. President Reagan stopped to wave at reporters and others standing outside the building. "Mr. President," shouted a reporter who wanted to ask a question.[1] Reagan turned toward the reporter and smiled. Jim Brady, the President's press secretary, stepped forward to help with the questions.

At that moment, six gunshots were fired from the crowd. One bullet hit Press Secretary James Brady in the forehead. A second hit Washington police officer Thomas K. Delahanty in the neck. As Secret Service agent Timothy J. McCarthy threw himself in front of the President, the third bullet hit the agent in the chest. The fourth shot hit the window of the President's limousine. The fifth bullet glanced off the door of the limousine and hit President Reagan under his left arm. The sixth shot missed.[2]

The men guarding the President moved quickly as soon as they heard the popping noises. Secret Service agent Jerry Parr shoved President Reagan through the open door of the waiting car and onto the floor of the back seat. Agent Parr did not yet realize that the President had been shot. As Reagan hit the hump in the floor of the car's back seat, he called out that he thought Agent Parr had broken his ribs. The President was in pain and was coughing up bright red blood. Agent Parr thought a broken rib had pierced the President's lung. He told Reagan's driver to head for George Washington University Hospital, less than a mile away.

President Reagan's car reached the hospital's emergency entrance in three minutes. The President was pale from loss of blood, and he was gasping for breath, but he walked into the hospital on his own. When he fell to one knee, a nurse rushed to help him. He was placed on a stretcher and wheeled into an examining room.

First Lady Nancy Reagan hurried to the hospital from the White House to be with her husband. Dr. Benjamin Aaron operated on President Reagan soon after Mrs. Reagan reached the hospital. After the operation, Dr. Aaron told Mrs. Reagan that a bullet had entered the President's body under his left arm. It had then bounced off a rib and hit his lung. It missed both his heart and the aorta by just one inch. (The aorta is the large artery that carries blood from the heart). The bullet made only a small slit in the President's body because it was flattened to the size and shape of a nickel when it hit the car. No one knew the President had been shot until his clothes were cut off and he was examined.

Agent Parr saved the President's life by getting him to the hospital so quickly. "If the President had been taken to the White House after he was shot instead of to George Washington Hospital or taken to a more distant or lesser hospital, I think he would have been in big trouble," Dr. Aaron said.[3] President Reagan was close to death when he reached the hospital.

Another reason the President survived the shooting

was that he was in good physical condition. At seventy years of age, he was the oldest man ever to be elected President of the United States. But the doctors who treated him said he had the body of a fifty-year-old. Although a section of the President's left lung had to be removed, he left the hospital in about two weeks.

President Reagan left the hospital on April 12. He continued to recover at home. A special exercise room was set up for him in the White House, across the hall from his bedroom. In the following weeks, he used the equipment so often that his chest size increased. He had to buy new shirts and suits.

A month after he was shot, on April 28, President Reagan spoke to a joint session of Congress. Aides wanted him to broadcast the speech from the Oval Office, but he wanted to appear in person before Congress at the Capitol. The President waved and laughed and said that he felt fine. Each time he spoke of Brady, Delahanty, and McCarthy, the audience cheered. (All three men survived. James Brady, however, was so seriously injured that he would never fully recover.)

President Reagan learned that the person who shot him was twenty-five-year-old John W. Hinckley, Jr., from Evergreen, Colorado. Hinckley was a confused young man who had fallen in love with actress Jodie Foster after seeing her in the movie *Taxi Driver*. He had likely tried to impress Foster by stalking a public figure, as a character in the movie had done. Hinckley had stalked

President Carter during the 1980 campaign. He went after Ronald Reagan when Carter was not reelected.[4]

Hinckley was captured at the scene of the shooting by Secret Service agents. He was later tried and found innocent by reason of insanity.[5] He was confined to a mental hospital.

Doctors and nurses who took care of President Reagan in the hospital after the shooting told of his patience and good humor. Reagan's wisecracks about his injury are well known. When Mrs. Reagan first saw him in the hospital emergency room, the President joked, "Honey, I forgot to duck." (The boxer, Jack Dempsey, made this comment to his wife after losing the heavyweight boxing title to Gene Tunney in 1926.)[6]

Just before his operation, Reagan said to the doctors and nurses in the room, "I hope you people are all Republicans."[7]

"Today, we're all Republicans, Mr. President," answered Dr. Joseph Giordano, who was a Democrat.[8]

When he woke up after surgery, President Reagan could not talk because of the breathing tube in his throat. He wrote a note to his nurse, quoting a W. C. Fields movie: "All in all, I'd rather be in Philadelphia."[9] In the recovery room, he also wrote, "Send me to L.A., where I can see the air I'm breathing!"[10]

Other Reagan notes written in the hours after the shooting were soon made public. "Can we rewrite this scene beginning at the time I left the hotel?" he asked. Another note quoted the late British prime minister

Winston Churchill: "There is no more exhilarating feeling than being shot at without result."[11]

Although he told jokes after he was shot, the President admitted he was afraid. "Can I keep breathing?" he asked his doctors. And, "Will I still be able to work on the ranch?"[12] The Reagans' home in California was a 688-acre ranch. It was named Rancho Del Cielo—"Ranch of the Sky"—for its location high in the Santa Ynez Mountains northwest of Los Angeles. Reagan loved to go to the ranch whenever he could get away from the White House. At the ranch, he rode his horse, cut brush, chopped wood, and built fences.

After he was wounded, President Reagan joked about his own condition, but he did not joke about the injuries suffered by the other three men who were shot. He kept his promise to keep Jim Brady on as press secretary. And he wrote a note to Timothy McCarthy's children, telling them how thankful he was for their father's bravery.

The attempt on President Reagan's life had far-reaching results. Economic bills the President wanted Congress to pass were probably helped along by popular sympathy. Polls taken shortly after the event, during his first nine months of office, showed that the public favored his economic policies by a two to one margin.[13]

When people heard that the President could joke about being shot, many saw him as friendly, likable, and sincere. Well-wishers hung a get-well banner near the hospital where Reagan was treated. The banner said: "Dear Mr. President. There ain't no republicans or democrats now. We are all family. GET WELL QUICK RON . . . We need you! [signed] America."[14]

It may seem odd that a man who had worked as an actor before becoming President would be seen as sincere by many Americans. Perhaps it was because, as Reagan said, he believed his own words. "When you go on that TV tube and you're in a close-up—that happens to be my business," he told Bill Boyarsky, author of *Ronald Reagan: His Life & Rise to the Presidency.* "I came from the camera business and I know one rule we had in Hollywood and you can't break it—that camera knows when you're lying. That camera knows when an actor really doesn't feel the line he is saying."[15]

The late Thomas "Tip" O'Neill, speaker of the United States House of Representatives under Reagan, once said:

> There's just something about the guy that people like. They want him to be a success. They're rooting for him, and of course they're rooting for him because we haven't had any presidential successes for years— Kennedy killed, Johnson with Vietnam, Nixon with Watergate, Ford, Carter, and all the rest.[16]

Like all Presidents, President Reagan had his own style of governing. He had several traits that helped his public image. These traits included his sense of humor (most often aimed at himself), a feel for such national concerns as self-reliance and love of country, and a talent for public speaking.

Ronald Reagan rides his horse at the Reagan ranch in 1981.

Weak points listed by Reagan's critics are that President Reagan left too many important decisions to his aides, appeared bored at government meetings, and did not always know the details about his own programs. "So poised in scripted settings, Reagan seemed uninformed about many of his programs," wrote Michael Schaller in *Reckoning with Reagan: America and Its President in the 1980s.*[17]

Whatever his shortcomings, for some Americans, Ronald Reagan was proof that dreams can come true. He rose from humble beginnings to the highest job in the nation. "The dreams of people may differ," Reagan wrote after he left office, "but everyone wants their dreams to come true . . . And America, above all places, gives us the freedom to do that, the freedom to reach out and make our dreams come true."[18]

2

THE DREAM BEGINS

R eagan family legend says that when Ronald's father, Jack, first saw his newborn son, he said, "He looks like a fat little Dutchman. But who knows, he might grow up to be president some day."[1]

From the day he was born, on February 6, 1911, Reagan was called "Dutch."

Ronald Reagan, the second son of Jack and Nelle Reagan, was born at home, in an apartment above the bank in Tampico, Illinois, population 1,276. His older brother, John Neil, had also been born at home, on September 16, 1908. Neil was nicknamed "Moon" after the popular comic-strip character Moon Mullins.

John Edward ("Jack") Reagan, Ronald's father, worked as a shoe salesman when his sons were small. Between 1929 and 1932, during the Great Depression,

Jack Reagan was mostly unemployed. As a Democrat, he campaigned for Franklin D. Roosevelt in the 1932 presidential election. When Roosevelt was elected, Jack was given a job directing government aid to the poor. Later, he was in charge of a local office of the federal Works Progress Administration (WPA). The WPA was one of the many agencies created by President Roosevelt to help people hurt by the Depression.

Ronald's mother, Nelle, did good deeds for her Protestant church. She visited prisoners in the local jails, tuberculosis patients in a hospital for the poor, and others she felt needed help. She was also a would-be actress. For fun, Nelle acted in local plays and gave drama and poetry readings. Sometimes her two sons performed with her. Her older son, Neil, was a talented singer and dancer, and everyone said he would become a professional performer.

When Dutch Reagan was three years old and Moon was six, the family began a series of moves. In 1914, Jack took a job as a shoe salesman at the Fair Store on South State Street in Chicago. Before the end of the year, Jack lost his job, and the family moved to Galesburg, Illinois. Here relatives helped him get another job with a shoe store. The Reagans rented a house on a pleasant tree-lined street. Collections of bird eggs and butterflies were stored in the attic by the owner of the house, and Dutch spent many happy hours looking at them.

In 1918, when Dutch was in the second grade, Jack

Jack and Nelle Reagan with their two sons, taken in Galesburg or Chicago, Illinois, in 1914, when Ronald was about four years old. From left to right: Jack, Neil, Ronald, and Nelle Reagan.

lost his job, and the family moved again. This time the move took them to Monmouth, Illinois (the birthplace of the famous Wyatt Earp). Here Jack found work as a shoe clerk in the E. B. Colwell Department Store.

In the summer of 1919, Jack was offered a better job at the Pitney Store. Once again the family moved, this time back to Tampico, to an apartment above the store.

In 1920, Pitney sold the store. He had promised Jack Reagan a percentage of the sale if he would stay until the store was sold. Instead, Pitney gave Jack a percentage of another business he owned, the Fashion Boot Shop. This business was in Dixon, 26 miles away from Tampico and about 105 miles from Chicago, Illinois.

On December 6, 1920, the Reagans left Tampico for Dixon, population 8,191. They arrived at their new home in their first car, a used model purchased from Mr. Pitney.

In Dixon, the Reagans rented a house on the north side of town. The two boys slept on an enclosed porch.

Moon settled in quickly each time the family moved, but it took Dutch longer to make friends. Dutch liked to be alone. He studied wildlife, drew cartoons, and read.

Dutch admired the cowboy heroes in Western movies. His favorite actor was Tom Mix. He spent every extra dime he could get on Saturday matinees. Radio was also a popular form of entertainment for Dutch. He liked to pretend he was an announcer, speaking into a broom handle "microphone." He also liked to make up stories and act them out. "The boy was growing into a dreamer," wrote Reagan biographer Anne Edwards, "and he found escape in worlds other than the drab flat on Main Street."[2]

Dutch loved to read, but he had poor eyesight. He held books just inches from his eyes when he read. He could not see the chalkboard at school, no matter how close he sat. Dutch did well in school, however, because he had a good memory for dates, names, and math tables. Mrs. Reagan finally realized that Dutch could not see well. She had him fitted with large, black-rimmed glasses that he hated. (As early as 1947, Reagan was fitted with contact lenses. They fit over his entire eye, and he said they were uncomfortable.)

Although Dutch and Moon worked at part-time jobs, they found time for sports and other interests after school. (During the summer of 1920, when Dutch Reagan was nine years old, he played football for the first time.) The skimpy wages the boys earned helped the family buy things they needed. The money also bought a few extras, such as ten-cent Saturday matinees or an occasional ice cream cone.

In later years, Reagan often remarked that his family was poor, but "We didn't know we were poor, because the people around us were of the same circumstance."[3] Until he was in college, Dutch wore Moon's hand-me-down clothes and shoes.

Jack Reagan was always looking for a better-paying job, but much of the money he earned was spent on liquor.[4] In his 1990 autobiography, President Reagan

Ronald Reagan enjoyed sports. Here he is shown in his high school football uniform.

wrote frankly about his father's drinking problem. He said that his father drank the most when things were going well for the family:

> Sometimes he went for a couple of years without a drop, but we never knew when he would suddenly decide to go off the wagon again and we knew that as soon as he touched *one* drink, the problem would start all over again.[5]

Although the Reagan family was poor, Nelle wanted her boys to go to college. Moon spent most of the extra money he earned, but Dutch began saving early. For the first two summers after moving to Dixon, Dutch worked as a caddy at the local golf course. One summer he worked for a construction contractor for thirty-five cents an hour. Another summer he was a laborer for Ringling Brothers Circus, earning twenty-five cents an hour.

During the summer of 1926, when Dutch was fifteen, he was hired as a lifeguard at Lowell Park, the local swimming beach on the Rock River. He worked twelve hours a day, seven days a week, except when it rained and the beach was closed. He was paid $18 dollars a week and all the sodas and hamburgers he could eat at the food stand. He held this job for the next seven summers, through high school and college.

When he graduated from high school, Dutch Reagan had saved $400 toward college. (Moon decided not to go to college after he graduated from high school in 1926. Instead, he took a job with a local cement plant.) Dutch admired a Dixon High School football hero who

Ronald Reagan worked as a lifeguard. This photo was taken at Lowell Park, in Dixon, Illinois, during the summer of 1927.

Ronald Reagan

had gone to Eureka College, so he chose the same school. Eureka College was a small liberal arts school founded by the Disciples of Christ Church in 1855. The school was located about 110 miles from Dixon, near Peoria, Illinois.

Dutch Reagan arrived on the Eureka campus in the fall of 1929. He made the trip with his high school sweetheart, Margaret Cleaver, a minister's daughter who would also attend Eureka. Dutch knew the $400 he had saved would not be enough to pay his tuition ($180 a year) plus living expenses. He convinced the dean and the football coach that he was a hard worker and a good football player. As a result, he was awarded an athletic scholarship to cover half of his tuition. The coach found Dutch a job washing dishes in a fraternity house to pay for living expenses and the second half of his tuition. He was also given a room at the house.

While a student at Eureka, Dutch Reagan spent more time on his interests outside the classroom than he did on his studies. He dreamed of becoming a football star, but Dutch did not make the varsity team until his junior year. However, he was a star member of the swimming team, and he ran track. He was also a basketball cheerleader, a member of the student senate, editor of the yearbook, president of the Eureka Boosters Club, and student body president. Reagan performed in plays as a member of the Drama Club. He also worked as a reporter for Eureka's school paper, the *Pegasus*.

As a freshman at Eureka, Reagan learned for the first

time the power of a good speech. In November of 1928, Eureka College president Bert Wilson wanted to save money by firing teachers and cutting some classes that juniors and seniors needed for graduation. The students learned that Wilson wanted to put his changes into effect while they were away on Thanksgiving vacation. They thought this was sneaky, but when they complained, Wilson refused to speak with student body representatives.

Finally, just before Thanksgiving vacation, the students called a meeting in the campus chapel. Townspeople, teachers, and most of Eureka's two hundred and fifty students were there. Freshman Dutch Reagan was a talented speaker, so he was asked to tell the students that they should demand president Wilson's resignation. When Dutch finished his exciting speech, the students voted to strike. They did not return to classes after Thanksgiving vacation. Eureka College president Bert Wilson resigned so life could get back to normal on campus.

The experience left Reagan with the belief that words could achieve great goals. "Giving that speech— my first—was as exciting as any I ever gave," he wrote years later. "For the first time in my life, I felt my words reach out and grab an audience, and it was exhilarating."[6]

After Dutch Reagan graduated from college in 1932 with a degree in economics and social science, he returned home to look for work. (His brother, Moon, had entered Eureka when Dutch was a sophomore and would graduate in June 1933.) Job prospects were slim when Reagan graduated. Because of the Great Depression, many people were out of work. Reagan could not count on help from his family because times were hard for them, too.

Though he still dreamed of becoming an actor, Dutch Reagan first had to earn a living. He decided the next best thing to acting was a job as a radio sports announcer. Reagan hitchhiked to Chicago to apply for a job as an announcer with an NBC radio station. He was turned down because he had no experience. He was told to try the smaller stations first.

Reagan was discouraged, and hitchhiked back to Dixon.[7] Several days later he learned that someone else had been hired for another job he hoped to get, as the sporting goods manager for the Montgomery Ward store in Dixon.

Jack Reagan told his son not to give up his radio announcing dream. He loaned Dutch the family car to travel the Midwest looking for work. One of Reagan's first stops was station WOC at Davenport, Iowa. Here he tried out for a sports announcing job by reciting, from memory, one of the most exciting football games he had played at Eureka. He won a temporary announcing job at WOC. Later he was called back to fill a full-time sports announcing job, with a salary starting at $100 a month.

Three months later, Dutch was chosen for a

sportscaster's job at WHO in Des Moines, Iowa. As a sportscaster for Chicago Cubs and White Sox baseball games, his name was soon well known locally. Baseball plays at Wrigley Field in Chicago, or wherever the teams were playing, were sent to Reagan over the teletype in Morse Code. He then described the action over the radio, just as though he was watching the game in person.

At twenty-two, Reagan had reached his goal of becoming a radio announcer. He had no way of knowing, then, that this was just the first of many dreams that would come true for him.

3

THE ACTOR

In 1936, Ronald Reagan saw a way to escape the cold Iowa winters each year. He suggested to station WHO that he go to California to cover the Cubs and the White Sox winter training camps. He could learn more about the teams, he said, and he could write stories that would keep the fans interested in the players through the off-season. WHO agreed, and Reagan was off to California.

Reagan's dream of becoming an actor had never died. In Hollywood, he looked up Joy Hodges, a friend and a singer from Des Moines who had won parts in a few movies. Hodges sent Reagan to her talent agent, who arranged a screen test for him. Reagan had to return to his job in Des Moines before the results of the screen test were in. Less than forty-eight hours after he returned to Iowa from California, Reagan heard from his agent. Warner Brothers Studios wanted to hire him. They offered him a salary of $200 a week, to start, which was a kingly wage in 1937. He quickly accepted.

Dutch Reagan had moved to Hollywood in June of 1937. In September of that year he moved his parents to California. One of the movie studio's first concerns was Reagan's name. Studio publicity agents did not like the name "Dutch" and tried to think of a catchy new name for the actor. Reagan hated to lose his family name, so he suggested, "How about Ronald? . . . Ronald Reagan?"[1] Studio agents liked the sound of the name. They agreed that it fit the twenty-six-year-old actor.

Movie actors in the 1930s signed contracts with the major movie studios. These contracts were much like the contracts today's professional baseball players sign with major league teams. The actors agreed to make movies for one studio, for a certain weekly salary, for a certain number of years. There were many conditions in the contracts that favored the studio. Actors were not always paid when they were not working. They could be fired for refusing a part in a movie, and they were not free to quit and work elsewhere before their contracts were up. Newly signed actors, like Ronald Reagan, usually made "B" movies, which were shown on week nights, or after an "A" movie at matinees. The big-name actors starred in the A movies and were paid more than the actors who made B movies.

In his first film, *Love Is on the Air*, Reagan played a

radio announcer named Andy McLeod. He had four days to learn his lines, and the movie was finished in three weeks. From 1937 to 1964, Reagan made fifty-three movies. Most of his movies were B films, but Reagan also played leading or supporting roles in a few A movies.

In his films, Reagan usually played the wholesome, all-American hero. However, his last film, *The Killers,* cast him as the villain. This movie was not a success, probably because fans were used to seeing Reagan as the nice guy.

Reagan and Margaret Cleaver, his high school and college sweetheart, had planned to marry. But shortly after he moved to Des Moines, Margaret broke up with him. She had met someone else, whom she would later marry.

The break with Cleaver was painful, but once in Hollywood, Reagan eventually began dating again.[2] Then, in 1938, he made a movie called *Brother Rat* with a blond actress named Jane Wyman. The two began dating.

On January 26, 1940, Ronald Reagan, age twenty-eight, married twenty-six-year-old Jane Wyman. A year later, on January 4, 1941, a daughter, Maureen, was born. On March 18, 1945, the Reagans adopted a second child, four-day-old Michael.

During World War II (1939–1945), Ronald Reagan took time off from his movie career to serve with the United States Army. The United States entered the war after Pearl Harbor, in Hawaii, was bombed on December 7, 1941. Reagan reported for military duty on April 19, 1942. He could not serve overseas because of his poor eyesight. He served most of his military service in the First Motion Picture Unit in Culver City, California. Reagan was assigned to a place nicknamed "Fort Roach" because, before the war, it was the Hal Roach Studios. The Fort Roach Unit made documentary and training films. The unit also trained aerial photographers for combat camera crews.

Reagan was discharged from military service on July 11, 1945, shortly before the war in Europe ended.

After his discharge, Reagan joined several groups that he thought were working to improve America.[3] In 1937, he joined the Screen Actors Guild (SAG), a union formed to better the salaries and working conditions for screen players. He soon became a member of the SAG board. Several social action groups were formed in Hollywood during and after World War II. For a short time, Reagan was a member of three of these groups: the Americans Veterans Committee (AVC), the United World Federalists, and the Hollywood Independent Citizens Committee of the Arts, Sciences, and Professions (HICCASP). Soon Reagan was spending more time giving speeches for all of his groups than he was on his career.

After World War II ended, many Americans feared that the Communist party wanted to take over key American businesses and organizations. Reagan believed that the film industry was especially at risk for such a takeover because movies could influence such large numbers of people.

Unknown to Reagan, some of the groups that he joined were thought to have a secret plan to help the Communist party take over in America. Reagan quit the AVC when he suspected Communist connections. He also resigned from the HICCASP when it was investigated by the Federal Bureau of Investigation (FBI) as a possible Communist front group. During this time, many actors and others within the film industry were blacklisted. This meant they were denied work because they were suspected of being members of the Communist party.

By 1947, the Communist takeover threat had become a bitter issue in America. A committee was formed within the United States House of Representatives to investigate anyone suspected of being a Communist. Reagan was one of many screen actors called to testify before the House Un-American Activities Committee. As president of the Screen Actors Guild, Reagan told the committee that the guild had fought the Communists within the group. He said they did this by making "democracy work . . . insuring everyone [in the SAG] a vote and by keeping everyone informed."[4]

As Reagan became more active in the politics of the film industry, he made fewer movies. At the same time, his wife's career sky-rocketed. Jane Wyman finally won the dramatic roles she had long wanted. In 1946, she was nominated for an Academy Award for best actress for her role as Ma Baxter in *The Yearling*. Olivia de Havilland won the award that year, but Wyman won the best actress award in 1948, for playing the deaf-mute woman in *Johnny Belinda*.

Jane Wyman did not share Ronald Reagan's interest in politics, and the marriage began to fail. According to Ronnie Dugger in *On Reagan: The Man & His Presidency*, Wyman said that it was annoying to "have someone at the breakfast table, newspaper in hand, expounding on the far right, far left, the conservative right, the conservative left, the middle of the road."[5]

"At home, [Reagan] was either on the telephone in conference calls, working with various members of the Emergency Committee or writing speeches," Anne Edwards wrote in *Early Reagan: The Rise to Power*.[6]

The Reagan's marriage was also strained when they lost a baby girl, born too soon in 1947. Reagan was hospitalized with pneumonia at the time and could not be with Wyman during her own hospitalization. The Reagans suffered separately. Finally, in June of 1948, when daughter Maureen was seven and son Michael was five years old, the couple divorced.

After the divorce, Reagan's children lived with their mother, but he visited them often. Reagan's father, Jack, had died May 18, 1941, of heart failure, but Nelle still lived nearby. Reagan spent Sundays with his mother. In 1981, biographer Bill Boyarsky wrote that Reagan remembered this time in his life as "a lonely period, a time of working and waiting for something better to come along."[7]

Though his personal life was in turmoil, Reagan's financial status had improved. His agent won a million-dollar contract for him in 1944. The money would be paid over a period of seven years, at $3,500 a week, for forty-three weeks a year.[8] Reagan continued to make movies. He soon settled back into the bachelor's life he had lived before his marriage.

About the time Ronald Reagan and Jane Wyman

President Ronald Reagan in the White House Rose Garden with his son, Michael, and grandchildren, Cameron and Ashley Marie, in 1985. After his divorce from Jane Wyman, Reagan did not see as much of his children.

divorced, a young woman named Nancy Davis came to Hollywood for a screen test. (Davis's mother was stage actress Edith Luckett. Her stepfather was Loyal Davis, a well-known Chicago surgeon.) Before she went to California to take a screen test, Davis had been living in New York, playing bit parts on stage. The screen test was a success, and she signed the standard new actress contract with Metro-Goldwyn-Mayer (MGM). Her starting salary was $250 per week.

Later in her life, Nancy Davis Reagan told this story about how she met her future husband, Ronald Reagan: She noticed the name "Nancy Davis" in a newspaper's list of Communist sympathizers in Hollywood. There was more than one Nancy Davis in Hollywood at that time, and the future Nancy Reagan knew a mistake had been made because she was not a Communist sympathizer. She telephoned Mervyn LeRoy, a director and family friend, for advice. LeRoy telephoned Ronald Reagan, the president of the Screen Actors Guild and asked him to help Nancy Davis. Reagan made telephone calls to set the matter straight, then called Davis to report. He and Davis met for dinner to discuss the situation. Reagan and Davis liked each other so well that they began dating. Nancy Davis Reagan would say years later that her life "didn't really begin" until she met Ronald Reagan.[9]

Ronald Reagan and Nancy Davis were married on March 4, 1952. Nancy made a few films after her marriage but soon gave up her career in the movies. A daughter, Patricia Ann Reagan, was born to the Reagans on October 22, 1952. When Ronald Prescott Reagan was born on May 20, 1958, the family was complete.

Ronald Reagan had to keep working to support his family and two homes—a house in Pacific Palisades and a ranch in the San Fernando Valley. Film offers had dwindled, so in February 1954, Reagan accepted an offer to serve as master of ceremonies for a nightclub act in Las Vegas. When the act finished its two week run, the Reagans returned home to California.

In the early 1950s, Reagan had learned that General Electric (G.E.) was looking for a host for a new television drama series, *General Electric Theater*. He won the job and began working for General Electric in September 1954. Reagan was paid $125,000 a year to host the show and act in several episodes. As part of his contract agreement, Reagan toured all 135 G.E. plants, speaking about Hollywood, America, and patriotism. General Electric hoped the tours would show its seven hundred thousand employees that their employer cared about them. The tours also helped promote the television series.

By 1955, Reagan's speaking jobs included community service groups, such as Kiwanis, Elks, Rotary Club, and the American Legion. Other interested groups also asked him to speak. By the time General Electric canceled *General Electric Theater* in 1962, Reagan had become a popular public speaker.

For his first G.E. tours, Reagan talked about

This photo of Ronald and Nancy Reagan was taken during Reagan's first term as President. The couple was married on March 4, 1952.

Hollywood. He said that movie stars were just ordinary people, with families and the same hopes and dreams as everyone else. Later he talked about "America the beautiful," preserving family values, and serving one's country.[10] Eventually he talked about those things in America that needed fixing, such as taxes and crime, and how changes could be made.

Reagan's speeches were full of humorous stories, mostly about himself. After each speech, he answered questions and visited with people in the audience. People told him they thought taxes were too high and the government was too large and too often out of control. Reagan had the same complaints about government.

Reagan had been a Democrat all his adult life and had often supported an increase in government programs. Now, after listening to his own speeches, he decided his opinions about reducing the size and role of government were more in line with the Republican party. In 1962, he joined the Republican party.

After *General Electric Theater* was canceled in 1962, Reagan was not out of work for long. He soon accepted an offer to host and act in another television series, *Death Valley Days*, sponsored by the United States Borax Company.

In 1964, while Reagan was making *Death Valley Days*, his long-time friend, Barry Goldwater, a Republican senator, ran against Lyndon Johnson for President of the United States. Reagan agreed to help raise funds for Goldwater in his campaign for President. He traveled California, giving speeches and asking for donations to the Goldwater campaign.

Reagan gave his Goldwater speech, titled "Encroaching Control," on television. Thousands of people called in after the speech, pledging money to the Goldwater campaign. The Goldwater speech marked the beginning of the end of Reagan's days as an actor and the beginning of his career as a politician.

4

THE POLITICIAN

In 1964, after Barry Goldwater lost the presidential election, Ronald Reagan went back to hosting *Death Valley Days*. About a year later, Holmes Tuttle, a used car dealer, contacted Reagan on behalf of a group of wealthy businesspersons who called themselves "The Friends of Ronald Reagan." The group wanted Reagan to run for governor of California in 1966. He would run against then-governor Pat Brown, a Democrat seeking reelection.

The Tuttle group had been impressed by Reagan's Goldwater speech and believed he could defeat Pat Brown. They also believed that running Reagan for governor would strengthen the Republican party in California.

Ronald Reagan's years as an actor and as a speaker

for General Electric had prepared him well for politics. As Lou Cannon wrote in *President Reagan: The Role of a Lifetime*:

> When Reagan moved onto the public stage in the 1960s, he keenly appreciated that his career had given him a head start in politics. He knew how to make a speech and how to deliver a punchline. He knew that it was necessary to look directly into the television camera without bobbing his head, and he knew how to give a concise answer that compressed easily into a fifteen-second sound bite.[1]

Reagan finally agreed to run for governor of California. His assets were that he had a name everyone knew, experience in public speaking, and financial backing. His youthful appearance was also helpful. Reagan was fifty-five years old in 1966, but he looked younger. His full head of hair was a deep brown, showing no signs of gray. (Rumors that he dyed his hair were never confirmed.) Reagan's excellent physical condition added to his youthful appearance. He stayed in good shape by riding horses, cutting brush, and mending fences on his ranch.

Those who favored Pat Brown in the race for governor hoped that Reagan's movie career would be a handicap, but it was not. Just as Reagan had won film audiences with his easy-going, friendly manner, he also won voters. "People who listened to Reagan tended to feel good about him and better about themselves," Cannon wrote.[2]

Governor Pat Brown tried to use Reagan's career as an actor against him in the campaign. But when the votes were counted on election day, Reagan received 58 percent of the popular vote to Brown's 42 percent.[3]

Reagan campaigned as a political outsider who could fix the mistakes made by the Brown administration. As soon as he was elected, Reagan began his government housecleaning. Some sources say that Reagan already had his sights set on the presidency and wanted quickly to create a record that would help him in a 1968 campaign for President.

Reagan claimed after he was elected that Governor Brown had hidden the fact that the state was broke. Early in his term, Reagan's newly appointed director of finance, Caspar Weinberger, revealed that the state was facing a budget deficit of $200 million.[4] (When government spends more money than it takes in, the difference is called the deficit.)

Soon after taking office, Governor Reagan announced a hiring freeze and a 10 percent budget cut for all state agencies.[5] There were few objections from voters when Reagan sold the state-owned airplane that had been used by Pat Brown. He also cut out-of-state travel by state employees and stopped buying new cars and trucks for state use.

Other cost-cutting measures were not so popular, such as deep cuts within the mental health system. In fact, Reagan was forced to restore mental health funds to pre-cut levels and to increase the state mental health care budget.

Many of the changes Reagan made in his first weeks

and months as governor were not popular. For instance, critics charged that some of the businesspersons hired to fill government positions were not qualified or had conflicts of interest.

Some decisions Reagan made early in his first term as governor were also unpopular. For example, he took a hard line in the late 1960s when students on several California university campuses rioted against government and college policies. He told students to follow school rules or get out.[6] This did not solve the problem and led to more demonstrations. In one instance, at the University of California at Berkeley in 1969, Governor Reagan called out three thousand national guardsmen against students who were rioting in favor of turning a section of university property into a "People's Park."[7]

Also unpopular was Reagan's request for a tax increase. He asked for and won from the state legislature the highest tax raise in California history.

Reagan learned to govern on the job. He made mistakes, but by the time his first term as governor was over, he had accomplished some of the goals he set. He ran for reelection as governor in 1970 against state speaker of the assembly, Jesse Unruh. Governor Reagan was reelected by a margin of 53 percent of the votes to 45 percent for Unruh.[8]

During his two terms as governor of California, Reagan's management style was much like that of a chief executive officer (CEO) of a large corporation. He

page 4

Executive Department
State of California

    (16) Consulting with federal, state, and local agencies involved in the provision and delivery of services of prevention, care, treatment, and rehabilitation of narcotics and drug abuse;

    (17) Providing technical assistance, guidance, and information to local governments and state agencies with respect to the creation and implementation of programs and procedures for dealing effectively with narcotics and drug abuse prevention, care, treatment, and rehabilitation;

    (18) Reviewing, at least annually, the State plan for coordination of drug abuse prevention functions within the State, annual submission to the Secretary of the United States Department of Health, Education, and Welfare of an analysis and evaluation of the effectiveness of the prevention and treatment programs and activities carried out under the plan, annual submissions of modifications in the plan which it considers necessary, and submission of any reports which the Secretary may require;

    (19) Coordinating all narcotics and drug abuse services and related programs conducted by state agencies with the federal government, and ensuring that there is no duplication of such programs among state agencies and that all agreements, contracts, plans, and programs proposed to be submitted by any such agency, other than the Regents of the University of California, to the federal government in relation to narcotics and drug abuse related problems shall first be submitted to the Health and Welfare Agency for review and approval;

    (20) Meeting at least every (3) months with representatives of the State Drug Abuse Prevention Advisory Council; and

    (21) Reporting annually to the Governor and the State Legislature concerning its activities for the past year.

<u>(DRUG ABUSE PREVENTION ADVISORY COUNCIL)</u>

The Technical Advisory Committee to the Citizens Advisory Council, hereinafter referred to as the "Council," shall assist the Secretary, Health and Welfare Agency, in carrying out the mandates of this Order.

The Council shall meet, at least quarterly, or at the call of the Chairman or request of the Secretary, meet and make

PRINTED IN CALIFORNIA OFFICE OF STATE PRINTING

Governor Reagan was concerned about drug abuse. This April 1973 document involves the creation of a drug abuse prevention council.

recommendations to the Secretary with respect to overall community, regional, and State planning and policy making in carrying out the provisions of this Executive Order. The Council shall be solely advisory in character and shall not be delegated any administrative authority or responsibility. Council members shall submit their recommendations and comments on the State plan and any revisions thereof. Statements at variance or in addition to those of the single State agency shall be attached to the plan upon its submission to the United States Department of Health, Education and Welfare. Council members shall serve without compensation and shall be reimbursed for actual and necessary expenses incurred in connection with the performance of their duties.

IN WITNESS WHEREOF, I have hereunto set my hand and caused the Great Seal of the State of California to be affixed this 25th day of April, 1973.

RONALD REAGAN
Governor of California

Attest:

Secretary of State

by_____
Deputy Secretary of State

said that he hired the best staff members he could find, set goals, then let his trusted staff handle the details to reach those goals. However, his management style was often criticized as being too "hands off."[9]

In *Reagan's America: Innocents At Home*, author Garry Wills describes Reagan's governing style:

> Reagan attended all cabinet meetings as governor (without presiding over them), and personally endorsed the decisions made there; but the staff worked out deals and compromises before the presentation of the mini-memoranda that formed the basis of cabinet discussion.[10]

Reagan found conflict "distasteful," Wills continues, and seldom argued with a decision supported by his cabinet members.[11] Since Reagan's style was to assign tasks to others, he was only as effective as the staff he chose. Many of the staff members hired while Reagan was governor would later work for him when he was President of the United States. During Governor Reagan's first term in office, William Clark became chief of staff. Under Clark, all state business was handled during cabinet meetings, using one-page memos outlining points to be discussed. Attempts to bypass the cabinet and go to Governor Reagan directly were discouraged. Cabinet members usually worked out disagreements among themselves without involving Governor Reagan.

During Reagan's second term as governor, Chief of

Staff Edwin Meese used the same plan as Clark. According to Wills:

> Clark and Meese brought order to the Reagan administration, which made it successful. As Reagan later said: "For eight years somebody handed me a piece of paper every night that told me what I was going to be doing the next day."[12]

He was criticized, but Governor Reagan's eight-year administration accomplished many improvements. He spent more than Pat Brown, before him, but he balanced the books (partly because of a huge tax increase). Under Reagan, California state universities began charging tuition, and the welfare system was reformed. He expanded and improved the water conduction system. This allowed California to raise crops that otherwise would have been impossible to grow in that dry state. Some said his system of assigning power to others strengthened the government because there were fewer channels leading from the governor to government agencies.

In *Reagan: The Man, The President,* Robert Lindsey sums up Reagan's years as governor:

> Long after he left Sacramento, a debate would continue over the Reagan years in California. His supporters would say that his record speaks for itself; that he had run an administration that was efficient, slowed the growth rate of government, and left the state in solid financial condition. Some of his critics would describe him as a man who is often unable to grasp the nuances of a complex problem and who, after all, is still a performer—the actor turned after-dinner speaker.[13]

Executive Department

State of California

FILED

In the office of the Secretary of State
of the State of California

MAR 2 9 1974

EDMOND G. BROWN Jr., Secretary of State

By _Nikki Case_

Deputy Secretary of State

EXECUTIVE ORDER R 50-74

WHEREAS, the involvement of young people in various levels of government has increased greatly in recent years; and

WHEREAS, the age for full voting responsibilities has been lowered to eighteen; and

WHEREAS, the State seeks to utilize the energy and abilities of its youth to the fullest extent; as well as provide for their greater involvement in the decision making process:

NOW, THEREFORE, I, RONALD REAGAN, Governor of the State of California, by virtue of the power vested in me by the Constitution and laws of this State, do hereby issue the following Executive Order to become effective immediately:

1. There is established in the Governor's Office an Advisory Commission on Youth. Responsibility for the Commission is assigned to the Lieutenant Governor with the State Office of Planning and Research providing the necessary staffing. The Commission will be composed of 15 members representing as closely as possible youth throughout the State geographically, ethnically, by sex and by population.

2. Nominations for appointment to the Commission shall be submitted by the League of California Cities, after consultation with the California Youth Coalition to the Governor for consideration. The Governor shall give serious consideration to these nominations along with nominations of other youth related groups. Members must be residents of California and not older than 25 years of age.

3. The Commissioners will serve a two-year term and may serve an additional term provided he has not attained the age limit prior to reappointment. Initially, terms will be staggered - seven members will serve for a two-year term and eight members will serve for a three-year term. Thereafter, appointees will serve two-year terms.

4. The Commission will meet at least every two months at places to be specified by the Commission. The first meeting of the Commission will be held in Sacramento.

printed in CALIFORNIA OFFICE OF STATE PRINTING

As this 1974 document shows, Governor Reagan wanted to get young adults involved in government.

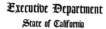

Executive Department
State of California

5. The Commission will be responsible for:

   a. Coordinating information regarding youth activities in the State.

   b. Fostering greater involvement of youth in all areas of government and encouraging the formation of local youth commissions and councils for the same purpose in addition to helping existing ones become more effective.

   c. Serving as the advisory group on youth affairs to the State Legislature and the Executive Branch of government, making such recommendations as the Commission may find necessary and desirable to carry out the purpose for which it was created.

   d. Conducting forums on areas of concern in which various governmental and non-governmental agencies and community organizations may be invited to participate.

   e. Studying problems, activities and concerns of youth in California.

IN WITNESS WHEREOF, I have hereunto set my hand and caused the Great Seal of the State of California to be affixed this 28th day of March, 1974.

RONALD REAGAN
Governor of California

ATTEST:

Secretary of State

by
Deputy Secretary of State

While Reagan was governor of California, a group of his backers began paving the way for him to run for President of the United States. In 1968 he tried for the Republican nomination for President but lost to Richard Nixon.

In 1976, Reagan was no longer governor of California. Now he could devote himself full time to campaigning for the Republican nomination for President. Again, he lost the nomination, this time to President Gerald Ford, but he lost by a narrow margin. Ford lost to Jimmy Carter in the 1976 presidential election and Carter became the thirty-ninth President of the United States.

Reagan's dream of one day becoming President began while he was governor of California. That his dream would come true was typical of his life. Just like many of the movie characters he played, whatever he had dared to dream had come true.

5

REAGAN'S FIRST TERM AS PRESIDENT

Ronald Reagan entered the race for the presidency again in 1980, after President Jimmy Carter announced he would run for reelection.

Reagan won the Republican nomination for President in July 1980 at the Republican National Convention in Detroit, Michigan. He chose George Bush, who had run against him for the nomination, as his vice-presidential running mate. Bush brought years of federal government service to the ticket, a qualification Reagan lacked. Bush had served as a representative to Congress from Texas, as ambassador to the United Nations, chairman of the Republican National Committee, chief of the United States Liaison Office in the People's Republic of China, and director of the Central Intelligence Agency (CIA).

In the election for President, Reagan won 489 electoral votes to Carter's 49. Carter received 35.5 million popular votes. Reagan received 43.9 million popular votes to become the fortieth President of the United States.[1]

During the campaign, Reagan had several advantages over Carter. One was the state of the nation's economy. Inflation (rising prices) had increased under President Carter, reaching a high of 20 percent a year by 1980.[2] In an effort to lower inflation, Carter's administration raised interest rates. This action caused unemployment to rise.

The 1979 revolution in Iran also worked against Carter in his campaign for reelection. In November 1979, Iranian militants captured the American embassy in Tehran. They took fifty-two American citizens hostage. Carter refused to meet the demands of the Iranians, and they would not release their prisoners. In 1980, Carter sent a small military force to try to rescue the hostages. The attempt failed when an American helicopter collided with a United States cargo plane. The plan was canceled.

Reagan also criticized Carter for supporting increased defense spending. Carter's signing of two 1979 treaties to return control of the Panama Canal to Panama at the beginning of the year 2000 was also used against him by the Reagan campaign.

Reagan took the President's oath of office on January 20, 1981. His inauguration speech dealt mostly with the nation's economy. In his speech, President Reagan promised to cut taxes and government spending. He also pledged to restore the United States to its former position of leadership among nations. "It is time for us to realize that we are too great a nation to limit ourselves to small dreams," he said.[3]

President Reagan's first official act on the day of his inauguration was to sign an executive order removing price controls on oil and gasoline. Shortly after noon on that same day, he announced that President Carter's efforts to free the captives who had been held in Iran for 444 days had finally been successful. The Americans were on their way home.

President Ronald Reagan with his wife, Nancy, seen at the inauguration swearing-in ceremony in Washington, D.C., on January 20, 1981.

SOURCE DOCUMENT

INAUGURAL ADDRESS

SENATOR HATFIELD, Mr. Chief Justice, Mr. President, Vice President Bush, Vice President Mondale, Senator Baker, Speaker O'Neill, Reverend Moomaw, and my fellow citizens.

To a few of us here today this is a solemn and most momentous occasion, and yet in the history of our nation it is a commonplace occurrence. The orderly transfer of authority as called for in the Constitution routinely takes place, as it has for almost two centuries, and few of us stop to think how unique we really are. In the eyes of many in the world, this every-four-year ceremony we accept as normal is nothing less than a miracle.

Mr. President, I want our fellow citizens to know how much you did to carry on this tradition. By your gracious cooperation in the transition process, you have shown a watching world that we are a united people pledged to maintaining a political system which guarantees individual liberty to a greater degree than any other, and I thank you and your people for all your help in maintaining the continuity which is the bulwark of our republic.

The business of our nation goes forward. These United States are confronted with an economic affliction of great proportions. We suffer from the longest and one of the worst sustained inflations in our national history. It distorts our economic decisions, penalizes thrift, and crushes the struggling young and the fixed-income elderly alike. It threatens to shatter the lives of millions of our people

Idle industries have cast workers into unemployment, human misery, and personal indignity. Those who do work are denied a fair return for their labor by a tax system which penalizes successful achievement and keeps us from maintaining full productivity.

But great as our tax burden is, it has not kept pace with public spending. For decades we have piled deficit upon deficit, mortgaging our future and our children's future for the temporary convenience of the present. To continue this long trend is to guarantee tremendous social, cultural, political, and economic upheavals.

You and I, as individuals, can, by borrowing, live beyond our means, but for only a limited period of time. Why, then, should we think that collectively, as a nation, we're not bound by that same limitation? We must act today in order...

On January 20, 1981, Ronald Reagan gave his inaugural address. Shown here is the beginning of his address.

On the evening of his inauguration, President and Mrs. Reagan attended eight, $100-a-ticket inaugural balls. Wealthy party-goers flocked to Washington, renting fleets of stretch limousines to drive them from one ball to another.

The 1981 Reagan inauguration set a record as the most expensive in history up to that time. The Reagans would later be criticized for the costly celebration, held at a time when inflation and unemployment were forcing many Americans to do without.

As President Reagan began his first term, top jobs in the White House were awarded to key players from his days as governor. Three White House aides—chief of staff, assistant chief of staff, and counselor to the President—were most powerful because they could provide regular access to President Reagan.

James A. Baker, III, a former campaign manager for George Bush, was appointed White House chief of staff.

Edwin Meese served as counselor to the President. This was a job with vague duties that was created by Reagan.

The assistant chief of staff position, also created by President Reagan, was given to Michael Deaver. Deaver was a public relations expert who had been close to both Ronald and Nancy Reagan during Governor Reagan's two terms. His duties included arranging the President's schedule and controlling media access to him. Often called the "troika" (a ruling body of three),

Baker, Meese, and Deaver played a major role in the success of Reagan's first term.

The Reagan campaign staff labeled their candidate's ideas the "Reagan Revolution." However, Reagan's political goals as President were largely the same as when he was governor of California. As President, he vowed to:

★ cut income taxes

★ reduce the size of the federal government and cut the number of government regulations

★ cut government spending

★ increase defense spending

★ appoint more conservative justices to the Supreme Court, and

★ balance the federal budget

Once in office, President Reagan's style of governing was also the same as when he was governor. He chose to take a broader view of issues rather than dwell on details, and he relied heavily on the advice of his closest aides. President Reagan concentrated on his role as the "Great Communicator," a title he had earned mostly because of his appeal to television viewers.

Governor Reagan worked from one-page mini-memos. As President, Reagan worked from index cards prepared each day by his staff. The cards contained his daily schedule, jokes and stories to use on certain occasions, and key phrases to explain his position on the issues. At times, the cards also had other cues, such as where to stand for photos during a ceremony. Reagan kept the cards in his pocket, where they were handy when he needed them.

Like many Presidents before him, Reagan did not often consult his cabinet. Although he claimed his cabinet was important, the only cabinet members who had much influence were those who had worked for Reagan before or were friends of his. Caspar Weinberger, a member of Governor Reagan's cabinet, was a powerful secretary of defense under President Reagan. David Stockman had great influence as director of the Office of Management and Budget. CIA director William Casey had served as Reagan's campaign director and was also close to the President. Later it appeared that Casey had a free hand to run secret operations. Treasury Secretary Donald Regan was also a powerful member of the cabinet.

Holmes Tuttle and others who had long supported Reagan served as a "kitchen cabinet." (This term was first used to describe the private advisors of President Andrew Jackson, who supposedly met with the President in the White House kitchen.[4] It refers to an unofficial group of advisors that the President consults more often than he consults his official cabinet.)

As soon as President Reagan chose his team, he began selling his plans to Congress and to the public. Reagan wanted to lower income tax rates. He believed that if more money was returned to taxpayers, they would save more. And if taxpayers put more of their paychecks into bank accounts and government bonds, more money would be available to the government and for banks to loan to businesses.

Cutting taxes was a major goal, but Reagan also wanted to cut spending on most government programs, spend more on defense, and balance the federal budget. These combined goals were labeled "supply-side economics" or simply "Reaganomics." The plan called for making up for the lost tax revenue by cutting billions in wasteful spending from government programs. Critics said the plan could not work for two reasons:

1. because money created by cutting taxes would not be put back into investments and business at the rates predicted, and

2. because cutting waste in government programs could not make up for all the lost tax money.

Even the President's budget director David Stockman expressed doubt about the Reagan economic program. In fact, as early as the summer of 1981, Stockman predicted "a minimum budget deficit of $60 billion for each of the next four years."[5] (This proved to be a low estimate. Annual budget deficits during Reagan's two terms in office ranged from $128 billion to over $200 billion.[6]) Still, Reagan was convinced that he could cut taxes, spend more on defense, and at the same time lower the deficit. The plan proved unworkable in practice.

Polls taken soon after Reagan was elected showed that the American public and the President disagreed on several counts. A February 1981 poll by CBS and *The New York Times* found that the public did not favor more defense spending over a balanced budget. Those polled were against large tax cuts. They also opposed certain budget cuts favored by Reagan, including cuts in social security, mass transit, pollution control, and aid to students.[7]

A Gallup poll taken shortly after the election showed that Americans also disagreed with Reagan on the Equal Rights Amendment (ERA) and abortion. Reagan opposed the ERA, but most of those polled were for it. Reagan wanted to ban abortions, except when the life of the mother was in danger. The majority of Americans polled were against any ban on abortions.[8]

Then, after the March 30, 1981, attempt on the President's life, the situation changed. Now pollsters reported a swell of support for Reagan. Influenced by the public's sympathy toward an injured President, Congress passed many of Reagan's programs.

In July 1981, Congress passed the largest tax-cut bill in American history. Although the bill cut taxes by $750 billion over the next six years, the cut was smaller than the President had requested.[9] Instead of the 30 percent Reagan asked for, cuts of 5 to 10 percent were to be phased in over three years.

The tax cut was largely offset by "revenue enhancement" bills passed in 1982, 1983, and 1984, which increased tax revenue.[10] The 1982 tax increase signed by Reagan was the biggest tax hike in United States history, calling for an additional $206 billion in taxes over five years.[11] From 1982 through 1984, Congress voted and Reagan signed laws increasing taxes on alcohol and tobacco. User fees were raised on many federal services. The payroll tax funding Social Security rose. According to Michael Schaller in *Reckoning with Reagan: America and Its President in the 1980s*, "Because of this and various state tax increases, the total tax bite for the average American family hardly changed during the 1980s, despite the hoopla of federal tax cuts."[12]

Congress also approved some of Reagan's first-term requests for cuts in federal spending. For instance, budgets were reduced for social programs, for education, and for regulatory agencies, such as the Occupational and Safety Health Administration (OSHA), the Environmental Protection Agency (EPA), and the Securities and Exchange Commission (SEC).

As budgets were cut for regulatory agencies, the number of business regulations were reduced. The effect of cuts in regulations was not all bad. Fewer banking regulations made it easier for borrowers to get loans. Deregulation of the airline, telephone, and trucking industries begun by President Carter led to lower prices during Reagan's term.

Congress approved increases in defense spending but not as much as Secretary of Defense Caspar Weinberger requested. Reagan especially wanted funding for a satellite warning and defense system called the Strategic Defense Initiative (SDI). When in place, SDI was supposed to give the United States advance warning of a nuclear attack. It would also destroy incoming missiles before they could reach their targets. Congress did not approve full funding because the project was still in the planning stage and, even if possible to build, would be costly.

Certain events that took place in the months following the assassination attempt made Reagan appear a strong leader. His handling of the strike by members of the Professional Air Traffic Controllers Organization (PATCO) is one example. On August 3, 1981, nearly twelve thousand air traffic controllers who belonged to the PATCO union walked off their jobs. PATCO leaders had asked the government for higher wages and better working conditions. When their demands were not met, union members voted to strike, even though, by law, air traffic controllers cannot strike. Although the controllers had valid complaints, such as outdated facilities and heavy work loads, President Reagan gave them forty-eight hours to return to work or be fired. When most did not, they lost their jobs. Some people thought Reagan overreacted when he fired all the striking controllers. Others believed he acted with authority to quickly resolve a difficult situation.

President Reagan's attempts to establish a friendlier relationship with the (then) Soviet Union added to his image as a strong leader. Relations between the two

SOURCE DOCUMENT

THIS MORNING AT SEVEN A.M. the union representing those who man America's air traffic control facilities called a strike. This was the culmination of seven months of negotiations between the Federal Aviation Administration and the union. At one point in these negotiations agreement was reached and signed by both sides, granting a $40 million increase in salaries and benefits. This is twice what other government employees can expect. It was granted in recognition of the difficulties inherent in the work these people perform. Now, however, the union demands are seventeen times what had been agreed to — $681 million. This would impose a tax burden on their fellow citizens which is unacceptable.

I would like to thank the supervisors and controllers who are on the job today, helping to get the nation's air system operating safely. In the New York area, for example, four supervisors were scheduled to report for work, and seventeen additionally volunteered. At National Airport a traffic controller told a newsperson he had resigned from the union and reported to work because, "How can I ask my kids to obey the law if I don't?" This is a great tribute to America.

Let me make one thing plain. I respect the right of workers in the private sector to strike. Indeed, as president of my own union, I led the first strike ever called by that union. I guess I'm maybe the first one to ever hold this office who is a lifetime member of an AFL-CIO union. But we cannot compare labor-management relations in the private sector with government. Government cannot close down the assembly line. It has to provide without interruption the protective services which are government's reason for being.

It was in recognition of this that the Congress passed a law forbidding strikes by government employees against the public safety. Let me read the solemn oath taken by each of these employees, a sworn affidavit, when they accepted their jobs: "I am not participating in any strike against the Government of the United States or any agency thereof, and I will not so participate while an employee of the Government of the United States or any agency thereof."

It is for this reason that I must tell those who fail to report for duty this morning they are in violation of the law, and if they do not report for work within forty-eight hours, they have forfeited their jobs and will be terminated.

Ronald Reagan made this statement in the White House Rose Garden on August 3, 1981, in reference to the PATCO strike.

countries had been frosty since the Soviet invasion of Afghanistan in December of 1979. However, by mid-1983, arms control had become a major world concern, and Reagan was convinced that the time was right to change the situation. Reagan had long been suspicious of Communism and had once called the Soviet Union the "evil empire," but he saw the need for compromise. With the help of Secretary of State George Shultz, President Reagan began writing and talking to Soviet leaders. This exchange led to summit meetings between the leaders of the two countries, during Reagan's second term.

Other situations during his first term gave President Reagan the chance to show that he was in charge.

On October 24, 1983, Reagan ordered the invasion of Grenada, a small island in the Caribbean located ninety miles north of Venezuela. The prime minister of Grenada had recently been killed by a group who then took over the government. The group claimed loyalty to Cuba's Fidel Castro and the Marxist government in Nicaragua. The Organization of Eastern Caribbean States, made up of six island neighbors of Grenada, asked the United States to use military force to stop the rebel military buildup on Grenada. Armed workers were building an airstrip on the island that the United States government feared would become a Cuban or Soviet air base, so without consulting Congress, Reagan ordered an invasion.[13]

The United States invasion was also planned as a

Received S S

1984 MAY -9 AM 10: 36

Andy Smith

400 London Pride Road

Irmo, South Carolina 29063

April 18, 1984

Dear Mr. President,

My name is Andy Smith. I am a seventh grade student at Irmo

Middle School, in Irmo, South Carolina.

Today my mother declared my bedroom a disaster area. I would like

to request federal funds to hire a crew to clean up my room. I am

prepared to provide the initial funds if you will privide matching funds

for this project.

I know you will be fair when you consider my request. I will be

awaiting your reply.

Sincerely yours,

Andy Smith
Andy Smith

This letter was sent to President Reagan from Andy Smith, a seventh grader in Irmo, South Carolina, in 1984.

JV

May 11, 1984

Dear Andy:

I'm sorry to be so late in answering your letter but,
as you know, I've been in China and found your letter
here upon my return.

Your application for disaster relief has been duly
noted but I must point out one technical problem: the
authority declaring the disaster is supposed to make
the request. In this case, your mother.

However, setting that aside, I'll have to point out
the larger problem of available funds. This has been
a year of disasters: 539 hurricanes as of May 4th and
several more since, numerous floods, forest fires,
drought in Texas and a number of earthquakes. What
I'm getting at is that funds are dangerously low.

May I make a suggestion? This Administration, be-
lieving that government has done many things that
could better be done by volunteers at the local level,
has sponsored a Private Sector Initiatives Program,
calling upon people to practice voluntarism in the
solving of a number of local problems.

Your situation appears to be a natural. I'm sure
your mother was fully justified in proclaiming your
room a disaster. Therefore, you are in an excellent
position to launch another volunteer program to go
along with the more than 3000 already underway in our
nation. Congratulations.

Give my best regards to your mother.

                    Sincerely,

                    RONALD REAGAN

Andy Smith
400 London Pride Road
Irmo, South Carolina 29063

RR:plr 5pmna
                        840511

HANDWRITING F

*President Reagan sent this typed May 1984 reply to Andy Smith,
concerning his letter.*

rescue mission to bring home eight hundred American medical students. The students were enrolled at St. George's University School of Medicine in Grenada and were caught in the middle of the local revolt.

Over nineteen hundred United States soldiers invaded Grenada. The island was quickly captured, the American students were flown home to the United States, and the mission was declared a success.

Public reaction to the invasion was at first favorable, but news blackouts and censorship kept the public from learning all the details of the invasion. For instance, nineteen Americans were killed; over one hundred were wounded.[14] A mental hospital had been bombed by mistake. There were bickering and serious communications problems among branches of the military. By December 1983, a Harris poll found that a 65 percent *majority* believed the Reagan administration had been wrong to keep reporters out during the Grenada invasion.[15]

During his first term in office, Reagan was able to get Congress to support a spending cut for most domestic programs and a tax reduction over a three-year period. His administration had assumed that the tax cut, by stimulating the economy, would produce increased federal revenues and a balanced budget. This did not happen. In fact, the national debt rose steeply during Reagan's first four years.

The United States economy suffered a serious slow-down (called a recession), lasting from 1981 to

1983. However, in 1984, inflation and interest rates fell, and economic conditions improved. By the time President Reagan was ready to begin campaigning for reelection, he could take credit for the revival of the nation's economy. The stage had been set for President Reagan to successfully run for reelection.

6

REAGAN'S SECOND TERM AS PRESIDENT

R onald Reagan and George Bush won an overwhelming victory in the November 1984 election against Democratic candidate Walter Mondale and his running mate, Geraldine Ferraro. Ferraro, a New York lawyer serving as a United States congresswoman, was the first female vice-presidential nominee of a major American political party. When nominated, she was head of the Democratic party's platform committee.

The Reagan-Bush team captured 59 percent of the popular vote.[1] Reagan received 525 electoral votes to Mondale's 13, for the largest electoral-vote landslide in United States history.[2]

President Ronald Reagan and Vice President George Bush were sworn in for their second term in office on January 21, 1985.

Reagan's goals for the country during his second term were largely the same as when he first took office four years earlier. At home, he would continue efforts to reduce federal spending and bring down the deficit. He would also push for more tax reform and increased spending on the military.

A major foreign policy goal for Reagan during his second term was to sign an arms reduction agreement with the Soviet Union. He also hoped to further peace in the Middle East and help prevent further Communist intrusion in Central America. In fact, it was Reagan's desire to help the Contra forces in Nicaragua in their fight against the Communist Sandinista government that led to a major scandal during his second term in office.

Improved economic conditions helped President Reagan win the election. As Reagan began his second term, the nation was gradually recovering from the recession, and inflation and unemployment rates had improved. However, private savings and business investments were down, and the gap between the richest and poorest Americans had widened.

From 1984 to 1988, successes in foreign affairs, especially in relations between the United States and the Soviet Union, drew public attention away from the sluggish economy. One reason for Reagan's success in this area was that he got along well with Mikhail Gorbachev, general secretary of the Soviet Union.

Gorbachev became general secretary of the Soviet

Union in March 1985, a short time after President Reagan began his second term. Gorbachev encouraged openness (Russian "glasnost") and democracy in his country. He also wanted to change Soviet social and economic systems. (Economic reform is known as "perestroika" in Russian.) Gorbachev's open attitude meant that he was more willing than previous Russian leaders had been to meet with President Reagan to discuss shared concerns.

The first meeting between Reagan and Gorbachev took place on November 19, 1985, in Geneva, Switzerland, at Villa Fleur d'Eau, a twenty-room mansion on Lake Geneva. At that first meeting, President Reagan

President Reagan is shown leaving the White House in Marine One, the presidential helicopter. With Reagan is his dog, Lucky.

SOURCE DOCUMENT

GOOD EVENING. As most of you know, I've just returned from meetings in Iceland with the leader of the Soviet Union, General Secretary Gorbachev. As I did last year when I returned from the summit conference in Geneva, I want to take a few moments tonight to share with you what took place in these discussions.

The implications of these talks are enormous and only just beginning to be understood. We proposed the most sweeping and generous arms control proposal in history. We offered the complete elimination of all ballistic missiles—Soviet and American—from the face of the earth by 1996. While we parted company with this American offer still on the table, we are closer than ever to agreements that could lead to a safer world without nuclear weapons.

But first, let me tell you that from the start of my meetings with Mr. Gorbachev, I have always regarded you, the American people, as full participants. Believe me, without your support none of these talks could have been held, nor could the ultimate aims of American foreign policy—world peace and freedom—be pursued. And it's for these aims I went the extra mile to Iceland.

Before I report on our talks, though, allow me to set the stage by explaining two things that were very much a part of our talks: one a treaty and the other a defense against nuclear missiles, which we're trying to develop. Now, you've heart their titles a thousand times—the ABM treaty and SDI. Well, those letters stand for: ABM, antiballistic missile; SDI, Strategic Defense Initiative.

Some years ago, the United States and the Soviet Union agreed to limit any defense against nuclear missile attacks to the emplacement in one location in each country of a small number of missiles capable of intercepting and shooting down incoming nuclear missiles, thus leaving our real defense—a policy called mutual assured destruction, meaning if one side launched a nuclear attack, the other side could retaliate. And this mutual threat of destruction was believed to be a deterrent against either side striking first.

So here we sit, with thousands of nuclear warheads targeted on each other and capable of wiping out both our countries. The Soviets deployed the few antiballistic missiles around Moscow as the treaty permitted. Our country didn't bother deploying because the threat of nationwide annihilation made such a limited defense seem useless . . .

After the October 1986 meetings between Reagan and Gorbachev ended without agreement, President Reagan addressed the nation with these words.

just a small part of the total nuclear weapons stockpile. However, the treaty marked the first time the two countries had agreed to get rid of an entire class of weapons.

Gorbachev dropped demands that the United States give up SDI, perhaps because he knew chances were slim the project would be funded. He also agreed to allow on-site inspections by the United States to be sure treaty conditions were met. The Soviets would have the same inspection rights in the United States.

When Reagan and Gorbachev said good-bye in Washington, Gorbachev invited the Reagans to come to Moscow in June 1988. At this meeting, Reagan hoped to sign a Strategic Arms Reduction Treaty that would eliminate more nuclear weapons. (The two countries still had over thirty thousand nuclear weapons aimed at each other.)

The Reagans arrived in Moscow on May 29, 1988, for talks that were labeled START, for Strategic Arms Reduction Talks. As his meetings with Gorbachev began, Reagan again talked to the Soviet leader about human rights and about tearing down the Berlin Wall. Reagan was encouraged because by 1988 a limited number of Jewish citizens had been allowed to leave the Soviet Union. The two leaders could not reach an agreement about sea- and air-launched cruise missiles or about chemical weapons. They parted on friendly terms, but a Strategic Arms Reduction Treaty was not signed.

In addition to the summit meetings with Mikhail Gorbachev, historians have said that during his second

President Reagan meets with British Prime Minister Margaret Thatcher on the White House patio in July 1987. President Reagan and Prime Minister Thatcher formed a lasting friendship.

term, President Reagan showed strong leadership ability in other areas. For instance, in April of 1986, he ordered air strikes against Libya because of the alleged support of Libya's leader, Colonel Muammar Qaddafi, for terrorist activities.

And in a speech at Brandenburg Gate, West Germany, on June 12, 1987, President Reagan boldly called upon Soviet leader Mikhail Gorbachev to tear down the Berlin Wall. "General Secretary Gorbachev, if you seek peace," he said, "if you seek prosperity for the Soviet Union and Eastern Europe, if you seek liberalization: Come here to this gate! Mr. Gorbachev, open this gate! Mr. Gorbachev, tear down this wall!"[5] (The Berlin Wall finally came down in 1989.)

In another incident, in February of 1988, President Reagan ordered the Justice Department to charge Manuel Noriega, the dictator of Panama, with drug smuggling. In 1989, after Reagan left office, his successor, President George Bush, sent troops to Panama to arrest Noriega and bring him to the United States. In 1991, he was convicted of drug charges and is serving a prison sentence in the United States.

President Reagan has also been noted for his compassion for Americans after a national tragedy. This was especially evident on two occasions during his second term in office. On December 16, 1985, President and Mrs. Reagan comforted family members of 248 American soldiers of the 101st Airborne unit who were on their way home for the Christmas holidays when their transport plane crashed on takeoff in Gander, Newfoundland.

The Reagans again comforted family members and the American people in January 1986 when the spaceship *Challenger* exploded shortly after liftoff, killing all seven astronauts on board. In his speech delivered after the disaster, President Reagan stressed renewal. He said the "seven *Challenger* heros" had "slipped the surly bonds of earth to touch the face of God."[6]

Tax reform continued during President Reagan's second term. On October 22, 1986, Congress approved and Reagan signed into law the Tax Reform Act of 1986. This law called for more changes in the United States

President Reagan and First Lady Nancy Reagan pay their respects to the seven astronauts killed in the Challenger *disaster.*

SOURCE DOCUMENT

LADIES AND GENTLEMEN, I'd planned to speak to you tonight to report on the state of the Union, but the events of earlier today have led me to change those plans. Today is a day for mourning and remembering.

Nancy and I are pained to the core by the tragedy of the shuttle *Challenger*. We know we share this pain with all of the people of our country. This is truly a national loss.

Nineteen years ago, almost to the day, we lost three astronauts in a terrible accident on the ground. But we've never lost an astronaut in flight; we've never had a tragedy like this. And perhaps we've forgotten the courage it took for the crew of the shuttle; but they, the *Challenger* Seven, were aware of the dangers, but overcame them and did their jobs brilliantly. We mourn seven heroes: Michael Smith, Dick Scobee, Judith Resnik, Ronald McNair, Ellison Onizuka, Gregory Jarvis, and Christa McAuliffe. We mourn their loss as a nation together.

For the families of the seven, we cannot bear, as you do, the full impact of the tragedy. But we feel the loss, as we're thinking about you so very much. Your loved ones were daring and brave, and they had that special grace, that special spirit that says, "Give me a challenge and I'll meet it with joy." They had a hunger to explore the universe and discover its truths. They wished to serve, and they did. They served all of us.

We've grown used to wonders in this century. It's hard to dazzle us. But for twenty-five years the United States space program has been doing just that. We've grown used to the idea of space, and perhaps we forget that we've only just begun. We're still pioneers. They, the members of the *Challenger* crew, were pioneers.

And I want to say something to the schoolchildren of America who were watching the live coverage of the shuttle's takeoff. I know it is hard to understand, but sometimes painful things like this happen. It's all part of the process of exploration and discovery. It's all part of taking a chance and expanding man's horizons. The future doesn't belong to the fainthearted; it belongs to the brave. The *Challenger* crew was pulling us into the future, and we'll continue to follow them.

I've always had great faith in and respect for our space program, and what happened today does nothing to diminish it. We don't hide our space program. . .

On the January 1986 night that President Reagan had planned his State of the Union address, he instead gave this address to the nation concerning the Challenger *disaster.*

tax system than any other law before it. The Tax Reform Act of 1986

- ★ reduced the number of personal income tax brackets from fourteen to three. The three brackets taxed personal income at 15 percent, 28 percent, and 32 percent.

- ★ raised taxes on corporations.

- ★ eliminated many tax deductions for individuals and closed dozen of loopholes. For example, taxpayers could no longer deduct state sales taxes or the interest paid on charge cards, car loans, and other consumer credit.

- ★ cracked down on tax shelters, such as real estate partnerships, that let people with high incomes avoid some taxes.

- ★ canceled the investment tax credit.

- ★ slowed depreciation allowances.

- ★ fully taxed capital gains (profits made when investments are sold).

- ★ gave elderly and blind taxpayers a double personal tax exemption.

- ★ removed some low income persons from the tax rolls by increasing the personal exemption allowed for dependents.

In the 1987 tax year, most of the nation's taxpayers found their taxes reduced an average of just $2.50 to $8

A grieving President Reagan ponders his remarks before speaking to family members of the seven astronauts killed in the Challenger *disaster, in January 1986.*

a week under the Tax Reform Act of 1986. In the same tax year, 17.5 million Americans, about half of those with incomes over $75,000 per year, found their taxes had increased.[7]

Despite some successes in tax reform and in United States-Soviet relations, a lingering scandal marred President Reagan's second term. As a longtime foe of Communism, one of Reagan's favorite causes while he was President was helping Contra rebels in Nicaragua fight that country's Communist Sandinista government. The Contras, whom Reagan called "freedom fighters," survived mostly on American aid, funded by Congress. Central Intelligence Agency Director William Casey used CIA agents to train Contra fighters and move aid and arms to them.

In 1982, Congress decided that the American government should limit its support for the rebels in Nicaragua. They passed the Boland Amendment, sponsored by Representative Edward P. Boland of Massachusetts, which capped CIA aid to the Contras at $24 million. The amendment also said that United States funds could not be used to overthrow the Nicaraguan government. President Reagan reportedly did not agree with the limits imposed by the Boland Amendment and encouraged his staff to continue to help the Contras.[8]

The Boland Amendment II was passed in October 1984 cutting off all aid to the Contras. This amendment clearly barred the CIA or any other United States intelligence agency from helping the Contras. Still, some Reagan staff members continued their efforts on behalf of the Contras. Besides CIA Director William Casey, other Reagan staff members involved in the Contra aid project included National Security Advisor Robert McFarlane and his chief deputy Admiral John Poindexter and National Security Council staff member Colonel Oliver North.

Another cause Reagan considered a priority was the release of seven American hostages, held captive by radical religious groups in Iran. The Americans had been working at various jobs in Beirut, Lebanon, and most had been captured when they did not heed the United States government's advice to leave the unstable city.

Through secret meetings and tactics worthy of a spy novel, McFarlane, Poindexter, and North hatched a plan to free the hostages without making it appear that the United States was making deals with terrorists. Under the plan, Israel would sell American missiles to Iran, using middlemen as go-betweens, in exchange for the release of the hostages.

As the plan unfolded, missiles made in the United States were sold by Israel to Iran at inflated prices. This was done with the authorization of President Reagan but without the knowledge or permission of Congress.[9] Unfortunately, no hostages gained freedom as a direct result of the weapons sales.

Although hostages were not released as hoped, the secret weapons sales to Iran continued. Proceeds from the sales went, in part, to purchase arms for the Contras. The plan was illegal for two reasons: First, it is illegal for private citizens to sell American government property for a profit. Second, the Boland amendments made it illegal for United States intelligence agencies to aid the Contras.

In addition to obtaining money through the sale of weapons to Iran, McFarlane and Casey used North to ask other countries to give financial aid to the Contras. Eventually Richard V. Secord, a former Air Force major general, was brought in to set up other sources of funds outside of the United States. North supervised the secret fund-collecting and fund-dispersing operation, called "Enterprise."[10] He made sure that money from the various sources was moved into Swiss bank accounts, then reached the Contras in the form of weapons and supplies.

The plot began to unravel when a cargo plane was shot down over Nicaragua and a crew member, Eugene Hasenfus, was captured by the Sandinistas. Hasenfus admitted that he was actually employed by the CIA. Now the plan, dubbed the "Iran-Contra Affair" by the news media, was exposed.

As details of the Iran-Contra affair were made public, several investigations began. The Congressional Joint Investigative Committee was formed by Congress and began televised hearings on May 5, 1987. At the same time, a New York lawyer, Lawrence W. Walsh, was appointed independent counsel to look into possible criminal acts in the Iran-Contra affair.

Reagan appointed his own investigative committee, the Tower Commission, headed by former United States Senator John Tower of Texas. The commission report, issued February 26, 1987, two months before congressional hearings into Iran-Contra began, found the President innocent of criminal conduct. However, the report criticized Reagan for his lack of control over the National Security Council. The report stated, in part:

> The President's management style is to put the principal responsibility for policy review and implementation on the shoulders of his advisors. Nevertheless, with such a complex, high-risk operation and so much at stake, the President should have ensured that the NSC system did not fail him. He did not force his policy to undergo the most critical review of which the NSC participants and the process were capable. At no time did he insist upon accountability and performance review. Had the President chosen to drive the NSC system, the outcome could well have been different.[11]

The secret operation bypassed all normal government controls. Poindexter, McFarlane, and North operated on their own to carry out actions that were expressly forbidden by Congress. When Congress inquired, they did not tell the entire truth about their activities.[12] When the secret was finally exposed, President Reagan pled innocence and ignorance of the details of the plan.[13]

The Congressional Joint Investigative Committee heard the testimony of twenty-eight witnesses over forty days of public hearings. In a report issued in November 1987, the committee found no firm evidence that Reagan had known about the diversion of funds to the Contras. However, it also found that the President was responsible for the way his policies were carried out by staff members.

Oliver North was tried in May 1989. He was convicted of obstructing Congress and illegally destroying government documents. His conviction was later overturned because the congressional investigative committee had granted him immunity from criminal prosecution in exchange for his testimony. A guilty verdict for Poindexter was also later overturned. William Casey died of a brain tumor before the investigation began.

In December 1992, President George Bush, who had served as Reagan's Vice President, pardoned many top government officials who had been charged or convicted for their part in the Iran-Contra affair.

Independent prosecutor Lawrence Walsh issued his final report in January of 1994. He found that there was no evidence that Reagan had broken the law. He added, however, that the President may have taken part in, or known about, a cover-up.[14]

As President Reagan's second term in office ended, the Iran-Contra affair served as a chilling example of what critics called his inattention to detail. On the other hand, Reagan could cite such accomplishments as tax reform, the INF treaty between the United States and

SOURCE DOCUMENT

MY FELLOW AMERICANS: This is the thirty-fourth time I'll speak to you from the Oval Office and the last. We've been together eight years now, and soon it'll be time for me to go. But before I do, I wanted to share some thoughts, some of which I've been saving for a long time.

It's been the honor of my life to be your president. So many of you have written the past few weeks to say thanks, but I could say as much to you. Nancy and I are grateful for the opportunity you gave us to serve.

One of the things about the presidency is that you're always somewhat apart. You spend a lot of time going by too fast in a car someone else is driving, and seeing the people through tinted glass—the parents holding up a child, and the wave you saw too late and couldn't return. And so many times I wanted to stop and reach out from behind the glass, and connect. Well, maybe I can do a little of that tonight.

People ask how I feel about leaving. And the fact is, "parting is such sweet sorrow." The sweet part is California, and the ranch and freedom. The sorrow — the good-byes, of course, and leaving this beautiful place.

You know, down the hall and up the stairs from this office is the part of the White House where the president and his family live. There are a few favorite windows I have up there that I like to stand and look out of early in the morning. The view is over the grounds here to the Washington Monument, and then the Mall and the Jefferson Memorial. But on mornings when the humidity is low, you can see past the Jefferson to the river, the Potomac, and the Virginia shore. Someone said that's the view Lincoln had when he saw the smoke rising from the Battle of Bull Run. I see more prosaic things: the grass on the banks, the morning traffic as people make their way to work, now and then a sailboat on the river.

I've been thinking a bit at that window. I've been reflecting on what the past eight years have meant and mean. And the image that comes to mind like a refrain is a nautical one—a small story about a big ship, and a refugee and a sailor. It was back in the early eighties, at the height of the boat people. And the sailor was hard at work on the carrier *Midway*, which was patrolling the South China Sea. The sailor, like most American servicemen, was young, smart, and fiercely observant. The crew spied on the horizon a leaky little boat. And crammed inside were refugees from Indochina hoping to get to America. The. . .

On January 11, 1989, President Reagan spoke to the American people from the Oval Office for the last time.

The Reagans depart Washington, D.C., on January 11, 1989, at the end of President Reagan's second term in office.

the Soviet Union, and the end of the Cold War between the United States and the Soviet Union.

As he said his good-byes on January 11, 1989, President Reagan told Americans, "I was not a great communicator, but I communicated great things." He added that the "Reagan Revolution always seemed more like the Great Rediscovery, a rediscovery of our values and our common sense."[15]

7

AN OVERVIEW
OF THE
REAGAN YEARS

P eggy Noonan, one of President Reagan's speech writers, wrote to her former boss in 1993 to ask him how he felt about the critics who were "trying to tear down his record." True to his nature, Reagan told her, "I'm not the sort to lose sleep over what a few revisionists say. Let history decide; it usually does."[1]

As is true of every President of the United States, Ronald Reagan's successes and failures will be debated by historians for years to come. Some have called Ronald Reagan a strong leader who restored Americans' confidence in the nation. Critics have stressed his ignorance of important facts and his apparent isolation from the daily workings of government.

Certain groups in the United States, such as African Americans, women, and environmentalists, gave

President Reagan low marks for knowledge and caring. For example, in 1982, President Reagan sided with two private schools, Bob Jones University of Greenville, South Carolina, and the Goldsboro Christian Schools of Goldsboro, North Carolina, in a lawsuit against the Internal Revenue Service (IRS). The schools had been denied tax-exempt status usually given to Christian schools because they practiced segregation, either in admitting students or in rules of behavior for students. In explaining his stand, President Reagan said later that he did not realize the tax problem was a civil rights issue.

The African-American community was also critical of President Reagan for opposing the observance of Martin Luther King, Jr.'s birthday, January 15, as a national holiday. However, when Congress passed a bill in 1983 designating the third Monday in January as Martin Luther King Day, Reagan signed the bill.

To improve his standing with African Americans, Reagan visited African-American schools and often honored African Americans of achievement. Despite these actions, throughout his two terms as President, Reagan did not receive high marks of approval from most African Americans.

In *Speaking My Mind*, published in 1989, Reagan wrote:

> For all my so-called powers of communication, I was never able to convince many black citizens of my commitment to their needs. They often mistook my belief in keeping the government out of the average American's life as a cover for doing nothing about racial injustice.[2]

SOURCE DOCUMENT

THANK YOU ALL FOR BEING HERE. And let me especially thank the Harlem Boys' Choir. From what we've just heard, I think that you fellows could show the famous Vienna Boys' Choir a thing or two.

But welcome, all of you, to the White House on this special day. Earlier today on my radio broadcast I spoke of Dr. King's character and contributions. Now let me speak a little more personally about the man who tumbled the wall of racism in our country. Though Dr. King and I may not have exactly had identical political philosophies, we did share a deep belief in freedom and justice under God.

Freedom is not something to be secured in any one moment of time. We must struggle to preserve it every day. And freedom is never more than one generation away from extinction.

History shows that Dr. King's approach achieved great results in a comparatively short time, which was exactly what America needed. Let me read you part of what he wrote from a jail cell:

"When you suddenly find your tongue twisted as you seek to explain to your six-year-old daughter why she can't go to a public amusement park that's just been advertised on television; when you take a cross-country drive and find it necessary to sleep night after night in the uncomfortable corners of your automobile because no motel will accept you; when you're humiliated day in and day out by nagging signs reading 'white' and 'colored,' then you can understand why we find it difficult to wait."

Martin Luther King, Jr., burned with the gospel of freedom, and that flame in his heart lit the way for millions. What he accomplished—not just for black Americans, but for all Americans—he lifted a heavy burden from this country. As surely as black Americans were scarred by the yoke of slavery, America was scarred by injustice. Many Americans didn't fully realize how heavy America's burden was until it was lifted. Dr. King did that for us, all of us.

Abraham Lincoln freed the black man. In many ways, Dr. King freed the white man. How did he accomplish this tremendous feat? Where others—white and black—preached hatred, he taught the principles of love and nonviolence. We can be so thankful that Dr. King raised his mighty eloquence for love and hope rather than for hostility and bitterness. He took the tension he found in our nation, a tension of injustice, and channeled it for the good of America and ...

It was a historic day in January 1983 when President Reagan signed the bill designating Martin Luther King, Jr.'s birthday a national holiday. He made these remarks that day.

Reagan claimed that this "charge" bothered him more "personally" than any other remarks made about his presidency.[3]

President Reagan was criticized by women's groups for not supporting the Equal Rights Amendment (ERA). Proposed as the twenty-seventh amendment to the Constitution, the Equal Rights Amendment was intended to outlaw discrimination based on sex. The ERA was first presented to Congress in 1923 by Alice Paul of the National Woman's Party. No action was taken on it until 1970 when the National Organization for Women (NOW) took up the cause. The ERA was passed by Congress in 1972 but died in 1982 when it fell three votes short of ratification by thirty-eight states, as required by the Constitution. Congress again considered the ERA in 1982, but it was not approved.

Environmental groups, such as the Audubon Society, the National Wildlife Federation, and the Sierra Club, disagreed with Reagan's policies concerning the environment. To these groups and others, Reagan appeared untroubled about the environment. The Environmental Protection Agency (EPA) had cleaned up just six toxic waste dumps by 1985. And when EPA director William Ruckelshaus wanted money to reduce the causes of acid rain, Reagan said no. Ruckelshaus resigned after just eighteen months at the EPA.

James Watt, Reagan's choice for secretary of the interior, angered many people concerned about use of public lands when he said, "We will mine more, drill more, cut more timber."[4] Watt offered a record amount of federal land to business interests for oil drilling and mining, but most of his plans were blocked by the courts and Congress. When Watt resigned in October of 1983, he was replaced by William Clark.

Many critics opposed the cuts in social services voted by Congress during the Reagan administration. They believed the federal government under Reagan did little to heal social ills such as teenage pregnancy, drug abuse, homelessness, and AIDS.

Cutting the number of federal regulations for some industries also caused concern. By the end of the 1980s, nuclear power facilities were badly in need of repair. The future safety of commercial air travel was in doubt. Deregulation in savings and loans institutions led to corrupt practices that would cost taxpayers hundreds of billions of dollars.[5]

Critics also said that the rich got richer and the poor got poorer under Reagan. Official statistics show that the number of Americans living in poverty increased during the Reagan years. According to United States government figures published in March 1989, the average family income of the poorest fifth of the American population fell by 6.1 percent from 1979 to 1987. Family income for the highest-paid Americans rose by 11.1 percent during the same period.[6]

Moreover, changes in tax rates made during Reagan's administration favored families in the upper one fifth of the income scale. This group saw their federal tax rates drop from 29 percent in 1980 to 26 percent in 1985. Families in the bottom fifth saw an increase in tax rates during the same time period, from 8 percent to 10 percent.[7]

Although Reagan had vowed to reduce the national debt, when he left office it had nearly tripled, to almost $2.7 trillion.[8] According to Garry Wills:

> The President who came in to cut spending increased it throughout his first term. He added as much to the national debt in those four years as had been accumulated in our national history to that point, so that one of every seven dollars spent by the government in 1985 went to paying interest on the debt.[9]

Reagan's administration was also marred by the Iran-Contra Affair and by alleged ethical and legal violations committed by some government officials. Several former Reagan staff members, including Michael Deaver, Edwin Meese, III, and Lyn Nofziger, were charged in ethical misconduct cases. Deaver was convicted of lying under oath to Congress about his lobbying activities after he left the White House. Nofziger was found guilty of violating the 1978 Ethics in Government Act, but his sentence was overturned on appeal. Meese was investigated for several alleged ethical violations, including taking bribes, but he was never indicted.[10] Scandals in the EPA and the Department of Housing and Urban Development (HUD) led to charges against staff members for favoring influential developers.[11]

Reagan's antigovernment, antiregulation position

and his hands-off management style were blamed for ethics lapses among staff members. Critics said the President should have realized what was going on and put a stop to it. In *The Power Game,* Hedrick Smith reported:

> At neither end of Pennsylvania Avenue was a strong code of ethics set by the city's two prime political leaders, President Reagan or Speaker O'Neill. Each tolerated laxity. Both were old-fashioned politicians whose style was rewarding allies and turning a blind eye to their darker sides. Reagan's easy tolerance was legendary.[12]

On the other hand, Reagan's secretary of education, William J. Bennett, has praised the President's leadership style. "Your critics always said you weren't a 'detail' man," Bennett wrote in September of 1995. "Thank you for that. What great leader is? There are plenty of people to handle the details. You knew instinctively that the President must above all lead."[13]

Despite some setbacks during his two terms in office, President Reagan's accomplishments are notable. He won high acclaim for appointing Sandra Day O'Connor—the first woman—to the United States Supreme Court. He dealt well with Congress and helped pass laws to stimulate economic growth, curb inflation, strengthen national defense, and increase employment (20 million new jobs were created). He bargained skillfully with leaders of the (then) Soviet Union. His efforts led to arms reduction agreements and helped

SOURCE DOCUMENT

The Mayflower Sept. 13, 1988
Dear Mr. President I am
J.T. Doolittle I am 8 years
old I was wondering if you
have basball cards if you
could get Micky Mantle,
Babe ruth, Pee Wee Rees,
Don Matingly Willie Mays
Roger maris, And any others
you can think of And if you
cant do that could you
maybe give me your Autograph.
other side→

Love J.T. Doolittle

1127 CONNECTICUT AVENUE, N.W.
WASHINGTON, D.C. 20036 • 202-347-3000
CABLE: MAYFLOWER • TELEX 89-2374

A STOUFFER HOTEL

Above is a letter from J.T. Doolittle to President Reagan, asking if the President could send him some baseball cards. Reagan did not have any baseball cards, but sent an autographed photo to Doolittle.

The autographed photo that President Reagan—"The Great Communicator"—sent to J.T. Doolittle, in response to his request for baseball cards.

bring about the end of the Cold War between the United States and the Soviet Union.

Although some Americans benefited more than others, Reagan worked to cut taxes and government spending. During his two terms as President, the highest federal income tax rates were cut from 70 percent to 32 percent. Capital-gains taxes were cut. Interest rates dropped, and inflation fell to less than 3 percent. President Reagan appointed the 170-member Grace Commission to find ways to cut the cost of government. The commission met for one year, then turned in a list of 2,478 cost-cutting suggestions. Thirteen hundred of the commission's suggestions were put to use, saving taxpayers $39 million.[14]

Reagan's skillful use of television often worked to his advantage. As an actor used to being on camera, he built a personal popularity that was a powerful political tool. Reagan earned the title "The Teflon President" because, like a stick-proof cooking pot, the sense of familiarity and trust he kindled in the public kept criticism from sticking to him.

U.S. News & World Report reported in January 1995:

> Reagan, a former Hollywood actor and television performer, believed a celebrity needed to create a special aura to keep fans interested. And he knew that any public figure could wear out his or her welcome by being too visible. So the Great Communicator rationed his appearances, had them scripted to the last detail and always tried to convey optimism and dignity.[15]

Despite the Iran-Contra affair, tax increases passed

by Congress and signed by Reagan, and ratings that sank during the recession, President Reagan's approval rating was 70 percent when he left office in January 1989.[16] This was the highest public approval rating of any President since Franklin D. Roosevelt.

After he left office, Reagan continued to be in demand as a speaker. He earned $2 million in 1989 for delivering two twenty-minute speeches in Tokyo, Japan. In September 1990, he visited the remains of the Berlin Wall. In November 1991, he joined President William Clinton and former Presidents George Bush, James Carter, and Gerald Ford at the dedication of the Reagan library in Simi Valley, California.

After 1993, President Reagan was seldom seen in public. One of his last public appearances was in February of 1994, when the eighty-three-year-old Reagan spoke at a Republican fund-raising dinner in Washington, D.C. "With all that's going on right now, I'm afraid I'm not going to run for president in '96," he quipped. "However, I have not ruled out the possibility of running again in 2000."[17]

In a "Letter to the American People," published in November 1994, Reagan revealed that he suffers from Alzheimer's disease, a disease that affects some 4 million Americans. The illness usually strikes between the ages of forty and sixty. Among the symptoms are memory loss, confusion, and personality changes. The average life expectancy of persons with the disease is from five to ten years, but many patients now survive fifteen years or more, due to improvements in medical care. Reagan wrote:

> At the moment I feel just fine. I intend to live the remainder of the years God gives me on this earth doing the things I have always done . . . Unfortunately, as Alzheimer's disease progresses, the family often bears a heavy burden. I only wish there was some way I could spare Nancy from this painful experience.

Reagan's letter ended:

> I now begin the journey that will lead me into the sunset of my life. I know that for America there will always be a bright dawn ahead. Thank you, my friends. May God always bless you.[18]

Reagan's daughter Maureen said in a 1996 magazine article:

> Dad's sickness hasn't been easy for my family, but it has led to some of the closest times we've ever shared. . . . Dad takes a car ride to do a few hours of work at his office every day, attends church on Sundays and plays golf twice a week. But it's the quiet time with family—going for walks, swimming or working jigsaw puzzles together—that gives him the most joy.[19]

In November 1994, *Time* magazine said that Ronald Reagan's recoveries from a bullet wound and from his surgeries for colon and skin cancer were "an inspiration to all, even those who disagreed with his politics.

"He may not be able to win this battle [with Alzheimer's disease]," the article continued, "but the way he's fighting it—with candor and courage—could be one of his most important legacies."[20]

Chronology

1911—Ronald Reagan is born in Tampico, Illinois.

1920—The Reagan family moves to Dixon, Illinois.

1928—Graduates from high school; enters Eureka College.

1932—Graduates from Eureka College.

1933—Begins job as sportscaster for WHO radio in Des Moines, Iowa.

1937—Takes screen test with Warner Brothers Studio in Hollywood, California; leaves Des Moines for Hollywood; makes first film, *Love Is on the Air*.

1938—Joins Screen Actors Guild.

1940—Marries actress Jane Wyman.

1941—Daughter Maureen is born; father, Jack Reagan, dies.

1942—Enters the military.

1945—Son Michael is adopted; receives discharge from the Air Force.

1947—Serves as president of Screen Actors Guild.
-1952

1948—Divorces Jane Wyman.

1952—Marries actress Nancy Davis; daughter Patricia Ann is born.

1954—Works as host for *General Electric Theater*.
-1962

1958—Son Ronald Prescott is born.

1962—Changes party registration from Democrat to Republican; mother, Nelle Reagan, dies.

1964—Gives Goldwater speech, titled "Encroaching Control;" makes last film.

1966—Elected governor of California.

1970—Wins second term as governor of California.

1974—Second term as governor ends.

1976—Runs for Republican party nomination for President; loses nomination to Gerald Ford.

1980—Elected President of the United States.

1981—Survives assassination attempt.

1983—Orders invasion of Grenada.

1984—Wins reelection as President.

1985—First summit conference with General Secretary Mikhail Gorbachev of the Soviet Union at Geneva, Switzerland.

1986—Second summit with Gorbachev at Reykjavik, Iceland.

1987—Meets with Mikhail Gorbachev in Washington; signs INF treaty.

1987—Public disclosure of Iran-Contra affair.
-1988

1988—Meets with Mikhail Gorbachev for fourth time, in Moscow.

1989—Leaves office.

Chapter Notes

Chapter 1

1. Laurence Leamer, *Make-Believe: The Story of Nancy & Ronald Reagan* (New York: Harper & Row Publishers, 1983), p. 308.

2. Nancy Reagan, with William Novak, *My Turn: The Memoirs of Nancy Reagan* (New York: Random House, 1989), p. 17.

3. Lou Cannon, *Reagan* (New York: G. P. Putnam's Sons, 1982), p. 403.

4. Ronald Reagan, *An American Life* (New York: Simon & Schuster, 1990), p. 263.

5. Ibid., p. 320.

6. Cannon, p. 404.

7. Leamer, p. 316.

8. Ibid.

9. Nancy Reagan, p. 11.

10. Ibid.

11. Ibid.

12. Ibid., p. 12.

13. Michael Schaller, *Reckoning with Reagan: America and Its President in the 1980s* (New York: Oxford University Press, 1992), p. 51.

14. George Sullivan, *Ronald Reagan* (New York: Julian Messner, 1985), p. 89.

15. Bill Boyarsky, *Ronald Reagan: His Life & Rise to the Presidency* (New York: Random House, 1981), p. 19.

16. Cannon, p. 407.

17. Schaller, p. 58.

18. Ronald Reagan, p. 28.

Chapter 2

1. Ronald Reagan, *An American Life* (New York: Simon & Schuster, 1990), p. 20.

2. Anne Edwards, *Early Reagan: The Rise to Power* (New York: Morrow, 1987), p. 43.

3. Ibid., p. 48.

4. Laurence I. Barrett, *Gambling With History: Reagan in the White House* (Garden City, N.Y.: Doubleday, 1983), p. 39.

5. Reagan, p. 33.

6. Ibid., p. 48.

7. Ibid., p. 61.

Chapter 3

1. Ronald Reagan, *An American Life* (New York: Simon & Schuster, 1990), p. 83.

2. Ibid., p. 76.

3. Bill Boyarsky, *Ronald Reagan: His Life & Rise to the Presidency* (New York: Random House, 1981), pp. 65–66.

4. Ibid., p. 68.

5. Ronnie Dugger, *On Reagan: The Man & His Presidency* (New York: McGraw-Hill, 1983), p. 10.

6. Anne Edwards, *Early Reagan: The Rise to Power* (New York: Morrow, 1987), p. 320.

7. Boyarsky, p. 72.

8. Edwards, p. 255.

9. Nancy Reagan, with William Novak, *My Turn: The Memoirs of Nancy Reagan* (New York: Random House, 1989), p. 93.

10. Edwards, p. 456.

Chapter 4

1. Lou Cannon, *President Reagan: The Role of a Lifetime* (New York: Simon & Schuster, 1991), p. 40.

2. Ibid., p. 41.

3. Ronald Reagan, *An American Life* (New York: Simon & Schuster, 1990), p. 153.

4. Ibid., p. 159.

5. Ibid.

6. Reagan, p. 181.

7. Bill Boyarsky, *Ronald Reagan: His Life & Rise to the Presidency* (New York: Random House, 1981), p. 147.

8. Reagan, p. 185.

9. Ibid., p. 161.

10. Garry Wills, *Reagan's America: Innocents At Home* (Garden City, N.Y.: Doubleday, 1987), pp. 320–321.

11. Ibid., p. 321.

12. Ibid., p. 313.

13. Hedrick Smith, et al., *Reagan: The Man, The President* (New York: Macmillan, 1980), p. 49.

Chapter 5

1. *The World Almanac And Book of Facts: 1996* (Mahwah, N.J.: World Almanac Books, 1996), p. 478.

2. "Carter, Jimmy," *Microsoft® Encarta® 96 Encyclopedia.* (Bellevue, Wash.: Microsoft Corporation, 1993–1995), CD-ROM disk.

3. Michael Schaller, *Reckoning with Reagan: America and Its President in the 1980s* (New York: Oxford University Press, 1992), p. 35.

4. Haynes Johnson, *Sleepwalking Through History: America In The Reagan Years* (New York: W. W. Norton and Company, 1991), pp. 70–71.

5. David Stockman, *The Triumph of Politics: Why the Reagan Revolution Failed* (New York: Harper & Row, 1986; Avon Books, 1987), p. 271.

6. Schaller, p. 46.

7. Johnson, p. 158.

8. Ibid.

9. *Information Please Almanac: 1995* (New York: Houghton Mifflin Company, 1995), p. 42.

10. Schaller, p. 47.

11. "Reality Check," *Business Week*, February 6, 1995, p. 4.

12. Schaller, p. 47.

13. Ronald Reagan, *An American Life* (New York: Simon & Schuster, 1990), p. 451.

14. Ibid., p. 455.

15. Hedrick Smith, *The Power Game: How Washington Works* (New York: Random House, 1988), p. 436.

Chapter 6

1. Ronald Reagan, *An American Life* (New York: Simon & Schuster, 1990), p. 331.

2. *1995 Information Please Almanac* (Boston & New York: Houghton Mifflin, 1995), p. 642.

3. Reagan, p. 13

4. Ibid., p. 699.

5. Ibid., p. 683.

6. Michael Schaller, *Reckoning With Reagan: America and Its President in the 1980s* (New York: Oxford University Press, 1992), p. 54.

7. Dale Russakoff, "On Bottom Line, Not Much Difference For Most Individuals," *Washington Post*, August 18, 1986, Section A, p. 1.

8. Schaller, p. 150.

9. Haynes Johnson, *Sleepwalking Through History: America in the Reagan Years* (New York: W. W. Norton and Co., 1991), pp. 289–292.

10. Ibid., p. 288

11. Congressional Quarterly, *Powers of the Presidency* (Washington, D.C.: Congressional Quarterly, 1989), p. 134.

12. Hedrick Smith, *The Power Game: How Washington Works* (New York: Random House, 1988), p. 619.

13. Ibid., p. 620.

14. "Iran-Contra Affair," *Microsoft® Encarta® 96 Encyclopedia* (Bellevue, Wash.: Microsoft Corporation, 1993–1995), CD-ROM disk.

15. Schaller, p. 179.

Chapter 7

1. Peggy Noonan, "Why We Already Miss the Gipper," *Newsweek*, October 2, 1995, p. 37.

2. Ronald Reagan, *Speaking My Mind: Selected Speeches* (New York: Simon & Schuster, 1989), p. 163.

3. Ibid.

4. Lou Cannon, *President Reagan: The Role of a Lifetime* (New York: Simon & Schuster, 1991), p. 531.

5. Haynes Johnson, *Sleepwalking Through History: America In The Reagan Years* (New York: W. W. Norton and Company, 1991), p. 172.

6. Ibid., p. 243.

7. David Hage and Robert F. Black, "The Repackaging of Reaganomics," *U.S. News & World Report*, December 12, 1994, p. 50.

8. Michael Schaller, *Reckoning with Reagan: America and Its President in the 1980s* (New York: Oxford University Press, 1992), p. 46.

9. Garry Wills, *Reagan's America: Innocents At Home* (Garden City, N.Y.: Doubleday & Co., 1987), pp. 368–369.

10. Johnson, pp. 184–185.

11. Cannon, p. 796.

12. Hedrick Smith, *The Power Game: How Washington Works* (New York: Random House, 1988), p. 270.

13. William J. Bennett, "Thank You, Ronald Reagan," *Reader's Digest*, September, 1995, pp. 74–75.

14. Congressional Quarterly, *Cabinets and Counselors— The President and the Executive Branch* (Washington, D.C.: Congressional Quarterly, Inc., 1989), p. 151.

15. Kenneth T. Walsh, "Rediscovering Ronald Reagan," *U.S. News & World Report*, January 9, 1995, p. 26.

16. Schaller, p. 179.

17. Tom Morganthau, "Ronald Reagan: Facing Alzheimer's Disease," *Newsweek*, November 14, 1994, p. 38.

18. Ibid.

19. Maureen Reagan and Nancy Lloyd, "A Valentine to my Father," *Family Circle*, February 20, 1996, p. 140.

20. Hugh Sidey, "The Sunset of My Life," *Time*, November 14, 1994, p. 65.

Further Reading

Boyarsky, Bill. *Ronald Reagan: His Life & Rise to the Presidency*. New York: Random House, 1981.

Cannon, Lou. *President Reagan: The Role of a Lifetime*. New York: Simon & Schuster, 1991.

———. *Reagan*. New York: Putnam, 1982.

Edwards, Anne. *Early Reagan: The Rise to Power*. New York: Morrow, 1987.

Kent, Zachary. *Encyclopedia of Presidents: Ronald Reagan*. Chicago: Children's Press, 1989.

Reagan, Nancy, with William Novak. *My Turn: The Memoirs of Nancy Reagan*. New York: Random House, 1989.

Reagan, Ronald. *An American Life*. New York: Simon & Schuster, 1990.

Sullivan, George. *Ronald Reagan*. New York: Messner, 1985.

Wills, Garry. *Reagan's America: Innocents At Home*. Garden City, N.Y.: Doubleday, 1987.

Internet Addresses

Ronald W. Reagan Presidential Library

http://sunsite.unc.edu/lia/president/reagan.html

Ronald Reagan Home Page

http://www.dnaco.net/~bkottman/reagan.html

Ronald Reagan Biography

http://www.frc.org/townhall/hall_of_fame/reagan/bio.html

Featured Speeches of Ronald Reagan

http://www.townhall.com/townhall/hall_of_fame/reagan/
speech.html

A Tribute to Ronald Reagan
(on his eighty-fifth birthday)

http://ctdnet.acns.nwu.edu/~tylerh/reagan.html

Index